WRITING FOR VISUAL THINKERS
a guide for artists and designers

VOICES THAT MATTER™

WRITING FOR VISUAL THINKERS
Andrea Marks

New Riders
1249 Eighth Street
Berkeley, CA 94710
510/524-2178
510/524-2221 (fax)
Find us on the Web at: www.newriders.com
New Riders is an imprint of Peachpit, a division
of Pearson Education
Copyright © 2011 by Andrea Marks

Acquisitions Editor: Michael Nolan
Managing Editor: Sue Apfelbaum, AIGA
Development Editor: Christina Wodtke
Copy Editor and Proofreader: Rose Weisburd
Production Editor: Hilal Sala
Indexer: Joy Dean Lee
Cover Art: ©Julio Torres Lara
Book Design: Andrea Marks
Ebook Design Assistants: Ben Cerezo, Kelli Reuther
Book Design Assistants: Anthony Armenda, Joe Carolina,
Morgan Harrington, Grace Noel
Research Assistant: Reid Parham
Podcast Editors: Evan Rowe, Eric Arnold, Michael John
Podcast Music: Masmöd

Typeface: Whitney designed by Hoefler & Frere-Jones

ISBN 10:   0-321-76745-4
ISBN 13: 978-0-321-76745-5

New Riders
VOICES THAT MATTER™
1249 EIGHTH STREET, BERKELEY, CALIFORNIA 94710
AN IMPRINT OF PEARSON EDUCATION

USER GUIDE

The print book is one way to read the content, but you can also read this book as an ebook, by viewing the enclosed disk on your computer. The blue words thoughout the book reference the hundreds of links that you can access if you are connected to the Internet. Ideally, it is best to view the print book with the digital version open on your computer, in order to activate the links.

The following information is intended for those reading this book as a digital download or from the disk included in the back of the book.

Reading a PDF ebook

It is best to read the *Writing for Visual Thinkers* ebook using version 8 or greater of Adobe Acrobat Pro, or Adobe Reader. You can download a free copy of Adobe Reader from the Adobe website [get.adobe.com/reader]. Viewing the ebook in Acrobat Pro or Adobe Reader will enable all hyperlinks and features to be active, including the built-in search engine and accessibility options for people with visual impairments. The Mac OS X application Preview may also be used, but does not offer the same functionality.

There are several viewing and scrolling options.
• Full Screen Mode allows you to go forward or backward using the arrow keys on your keyboard, or by clicking on the far left or far right side of your screen.
• Reading Mode allows you to navigate by using the scroll bar or arrows on the right side of your screen; you can also use the up/down arrow keys on your keyboard.
• Normal Mode permits all methods of navigation (make sure your Page Navigation toolbar is in view). You can move forward, backward, up, or down either by using the arrow keys on your keyboard, or by clicking on the arrows at the bottom right corner of the page. You can also select the hand tool if you wish to manually move the page in any direction as you read. Acrobat Reader also allows you to type in a specific page number to jump directly to that page and add bookmarks at your favorite places.

In lieu of a traditional index, the ebook utilizes the search function. To access the search function, view the document at a comfortable reading percentage (such as 150%) and open the search palette either by typing your phrase into the navigation window (make sure your Find toolbar is active) or selecting Search, under the Edit menu. The basic search palette will allow you to type in a word you are searching for; advanced search options will allow you to type in either a word or a phrase.

Accessing links

As mentioned, hyperlinks require an Internet connection.

The first time you click on a blue hyperlink, your default browser will open to the corresponding webpage. Your book will remain open in the background and you can click on the PDF window to return to it. Most of the URLs throughout this book link to Wikipedia or another specific website, but some may link to YouTube videos.

Disclaimer: Though user-generated Wikipedia has become a standard tool for compiling information on the Internet, the accuracy of Wikipedia sites has not been definitively measured. Further research, using books and periodicals, can help bring a richer and sometimes more accurate understanding of the topic.

Due to the changing nature of the web, links may change. For technical issues, including broken links, please send an e-mail that includes the title and ISBN and describes the specific issue to ask@peachpit.com.

Your account

Register your ebook at www.peachpit.com/register to gain access to audio and video podcasts, and supplemental PDFs. After you create your account and enter the ISBN, the ebook will be listed under Registered Products on your Account page with a link to the content. Be sure to bookmark your Account page and save your Peachpit.com password to access future updates for this ebook. You'll also be able to receive discount coupons for future purchases from Peachpit Press.

To my students who have inspired me with their never-ending passion for design and writing: I thank you for your willingness to experiment with all kinds of writing in the classroom.

(The digital revolution has created almost unlimited resources for communication, and has brought the visual and verbal together in exciting ways while expanding the meaning of literacy. The 21st century is becoming a conversation about language, expression, and meaning. Join this exciting conversation and explore the many ways you can bring in writing to enrich your work.)

The tradition of writing in the field of design—whether serving as criticism, personal expression or persuasion—is long and storied. The design profession would surely be diminished without those defining voices—Rand, Glaser, Lupton, Bierut, Heller, to name but a few—that continually remind us and the rest of the world why the work of designers is so important. The need for designers to be able to communicate not only visually but also verbally has only grown over the years, to the extent that no professional designer today can afford not to develop the necessary skills.

With *Writing for Visual Thinkers*, a new voice in design has emerged. Writer, designer and educator Andrea Marks skillfully imparts her knowledge about the unique ways in which designers see the world and shows us how we can translate our visual ideas into words that are just as compelling and thoughtful. AIGA, the professional association for design, eagerly supports this ambitious educational tool for designers and visual artists, with the hope that it will benefit readers in their career pursuits and personal growth, and create ever more unique and inspiring voices.

I can't think of a single well-known designer who doesn't write well. Try this exercise yourself: name five designers you admire. My list includes Paula Scher, Marian Bantjes, Stefan Sagmeister, Abbott Miller, and Maira Kalman. All these designers know how to use words, infusing their visual work with verbal energy and ideas as well as communicating about what they do to a variety of audiences. They all have published books or essays about their own work as well as about bigger issues in the world of design. They all know how to speak in public about what they do. They all use writing to conduct their daily business as well as to do something bigger: build the discourse of graphic design. They have taken part in an ongoing conversation about design that stretches back into history and pushes ahead toward the future. That conversation is constructed with words as well as with visual evidence.

The same thought experiment would hold true for many other disciplines as well. Prominent surgeons, lawyers, architects, or filmmakers are likely to be strong writers, equipped to use words to discover ideas, hone their personal intelligence, and share their work with others. Writing can help anyone win friends and influence people. You can use words to get a job, apply for a grant, teach a class, win a competitive bid, or make a presentation. While you're at it, jump in and help build the discourse: publish a blog, review a font, or advocate for change.

Beyond its universal utility to any professional or creative undertaking, writing lies at the very heart of graphic design. Indeed, words are the designer's single most ubiquitous raw material. Nearly every graphic design task includes text somewhere in its development. Books, magazines, websites, branding, signage: designing these media requires shaping and understanding verbal content. Even a purportedly non-verbal icon system requires consideration of semantics and vocabulary.

Despite writing's huge importance to what we do, some designers approach the task with anxiety. Many of us associate writing with the drudgery of high school civics or college art history. What student hasn't padded out a research paper with big type and extra words in order to quickly get through an assignment? This mindset sees "the teacher" as one's ultimate audience. And how lame is that? Teachers are paid to read whatever drivel a student sends their way. In real life, readers must be wined and wooed before trudging willingly through any text.

I often hear students say, "I'm just not a writer." Alas, hiding from writing is no wise strategy in today's world. Frankly, if you can't write, you're not truly literate, because literacy requires the ability to generate text as well as to consume it. For those who remain afraid of this fundamental skill, *Writing for Visual Thinkers* will come as a warm and open-hearted invitation. This book is not a didactic, rule-mongering guide to grammar but rather an upbeat exploration of fun, engaging techniques for using words to unleash the powers of the mind. The book starts out with exercises for getting ideas; many of these involve working in relaxed group settings. This easy-going book carries the reader forward to more structured tasks, from revising an essay to publishing a zine. As author Andrea Marks explains, learning to write well will help you become a better visual thinker. Likewise, visual thinkers can blossom into fine writers, drawing on their sense of color, texture, and structural conciseness to craft sentences and paragraphs that use vivid, compact language to tell a story.

Writing for Visual Thinkers presents ideas and methods that can help visual thinkers become better writers. It covers topics such as 21st century literacy, the workings of the brain and its connection to creativity, and how to use writing in more pragmatic ways, including a list of resources pertinent to writing, art, and design. The book is not intended to cover traditional writing and grammar conventions, as many excellent books exist. (The latest edition of Strunk and White's *The Elements of Style*, beautifully illustrated by Maira Kalman, is a wonderful resource.) Instead, the goal of this book is to explore the potential of written communication as a way to better understand the process of visual communication.

"The art of writing is the art of discovering what you believe."

Gustave Flaubert

CONTENTS

THE WRITER'S TOOLBOX

1

THE WRITER'S TOOLBOX

Writing can be a powerful tool when you are creating visual projects. From initial notes and sketches to freewriting and mind mapping, writing can help generate lively, lateral thinking.[1] Writing helps to work through the process phase of a visual project, and can also serve as a reflective tool once a project is completed.

Writing begins as a private act that can lead to a more public expression. Writing during idea generation can be a way to gain comfort and skills that lead to better, clearer communication. Using private, "process" writing makes visual projects conceptually stronger, which ultimately leads to stronger "public" writing of materials such as proposals, project briefs, cover letters, and even blog entries and comments.

This chapter serves as a guide in using writing to enhance the creative process, both for visual and verbal projects. It presents approaches that use writing to generate ideas, support process, and reflect on finished work. These strategies are diverse enough to allow for different styles of thinking and learning. Some of these tools, such as mind maps, take advantage of words, pictures, and symbols; others, such as freewriting, focus on narrative thoughts. However, all of them use writing to bring out ideas in creative problem-solving.

"Learning never exhausts the mind"

Leonardo da Vinci

Leonardo da Vinci's 15th century sketchbooks are filled with diagrammatic sketches that could be the precursors of today's brainstorm webs, concept maps, or mind maps. Da Vinci's creative genius is revealed in the way his knowledge of art and science informed each other. He used left and right hemispheres in "whole brain" interdependent thinking to realize so many of his remarkable accomplishments.[2] The sketchbooks and notebooks of many other creative geniuses, such as Pablo Picasso, Paul Klee, Thomas Edison, Charles Darwin, and Albert Einstein, also show diagrammatic sketching that is similar to the mapping methods used today.

MIND MAPS

A mind map[3] gives visual form to ideas. It is particularly helpful for initiating ideas in a project. For visual thinkers, the diagramming of words in a visual, intuitive manner takes advantage of the more nonlinear, associative way that our brains naturally generate ideas. Like many brainstorming methods, mind maps needn't be questioned until they are completed. The goal is to develop the diagram quickly, then synthesize possible connections and directions. It may be useful to construct mind maps during particular phases in a project, when new connections and ideas are needed. Larger projects, which involve complex systems of information, also benefit from using these techniques.

In addition to words, another tactic for visual thinkers is the inclusion of color, images, and even dimension into these diagrammatic maps. These brainstorming techniques are varied and can help to better organize ideas and manage complex problems.

As with any new problem-solving or brainstorming technique, mind mapping takes practice. Look at it as one of many ways to explore an idea or understand a topic.

How mind maps work

Traditional mind maps are written by hand with pen or pencil, but many software programs and web-based mapping tools are also available. These maps can be done individually or as a group.

Handwritten mind maps allow for the quick, spontaneous flow of thoughts. Writing these diagrams on large sheets of paper, such as giant sticky notes or newsprint sketchpads, lets the mind map evolve and grow. Often, participants will become so engrossed that they are surprised when they reach the edge of the paper. Large mind maps can be pinned on the wall for further discussion and analysis.

Web-based mind-mapping software—such as FreeMind, and MindMeister—allows for the addition of links, notes, or files to specific words. All of these web-based programs enable both individual and collaborative diagramming and mapping of problems, and are simple and intuitive to use. A great feature of these programs is that real-time collaboration can take place from multiple computers in different locations.

Developing a mind map with words

Begin with a sheet of blank paper that is tabloid size (11"x17") or larger (particularly useful for collaborative mind mapping). Write a word in the middle of the page that best represents a central topic, subject, or question. You can think of this word as the "whole" in relation to the sum of the mind map's "parts."

From this central word, draw six or seven branching lines and at the end of each, quickly write one-word associations that relate to this center word. Nouns may be a good choice, as they usually carry more associations than verbs or adjectives do.

Circle each word and continue the creation of more branches from each of them. As you move further away from the center, your words will begin to have weaker associations with the center word, but new associations will most likely allow for new concepts to develop. Don't be concerned if the words eventually lead you far off your initial topic—that divergence can lead to new ideas.

Developing a mind map with images

A graphic mind map works similarly to a verbal mind map, but allows for the addition of icons, images, and symbols. Visual thinkers, comfortable with schematic sketching, may find the combination of words and images useful in developing new associations. Follow the steps in the previous description of a mind map, but use icons or images instead of, or in addition to, words. Add new symbols, such as arrows, lines, and shapes, to further emphasize connections. Hierarchy (varying sizes, weights, and colors) can also help to emphasize concepts and make associations.

Examining the results

When you are finished with your mind map, take some time to reflect on the results. If you are working with a small group, discuss the ideas that came forth and write or map out this conversation.

» Are there certain patterns and relationships that emerge?
» Are there new concepts that need to be considered and remapped?

If several people create mind maps on a similar topic, you can compare them. In areas of similarity, you may see patterns that can be used to develop a concept. Areas of difference might prompt further exploration through research and conversation.

CONCEPT MAPS

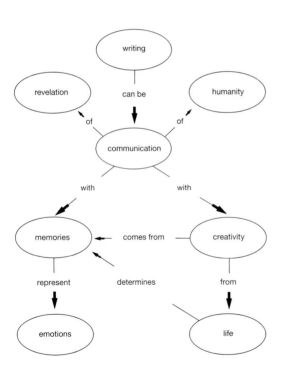

In many ways, concept maps are similar to mind maps. They too make use of associative relationships, using a nodal diagram containing words. The main difference between them is that concept mapping allows for a more thorough investigation and analysis of conceptual relationships and meanings. With the addition of propositional links, indicating relationships between two concepts, concept maps focus more on systems thinking.

Joseph Novak, author of the book *Learning How to Learn*, developed the technique of concept mapping at Cornell University in the 1970s, as an aid to science learning. As Novak states, "When concept maps are conscientiously constructed, they are remarkably revealing of students' cognition organization." His mapping techniques are used by students starting as early as first grade, and proceeding through higher education.[4]

How concept maps work

Concept maps show relationships of concepts (objects, people, environments, events, etc.) in a hierarchical order, from general to specific. Each of these words is joined by a proposition or linking statement, such as "depends on," "can be," "made of," "from." These propositional statements are the necessary links to create systems of meaning within the map.

Developing a concept map

Begin by writing the concept you want to explore at the top of your sheet of paper.

Next, continue writing related concept words connected by simple propositional phrases. For example, if the concept to be explored is "water," then below the word "water" you might write "living things" and connect the two by the propositional phrase "needed by." Meredith Davis and Hugh Dubberly depart from the traditional concept map and use a more narrative written structure, without a top-to-bottom hierarchy. Dubberly's concept map of the word "play," a project developed for The Institute for the Creative Process at the Alberta College of Art + Design, shows the many ways that the concept of play can be explained in a narrative, diagrammatic form. The poster combines narrative phrases, words, and diagrammatic symbols in a visually dynamic example of a concept map. Davis uses concept maps in her first-semester graphic design course at North Carolina State University. Each student is assigned an object (iPod, household appliance, t-shirt, etc.) and Davis provides a base map template. This template allows students to see the "situatedness" of an everyday object within larger contexts (technological, physical, social/cultural, cognitive), to articulate cause and effect relationships within a system, and to identify places for design intervention. The maps are points of departure for deeper investigations of the object, through writing and designing. The decision to place the subject to be explored in the center of the diagram allows for several concepts of similar hierarchical importance to be shown. The concepts become more specific as they leave the center node. As Davis states, "I use [concept maps] as narratives, so there is value in the connecting phrases being descriptive and smaller structures being captured within zones of the diagram. It is easy to deploy these structures as ways of organizing students' written arguments."[5]

When concept maps are expanded to include narrative writing, students are able to make more meaningful connections. According to Davis, "if it is just a reflection of how students view the hierarchical relationships among simple things, it is tough to make the writing do more than reveal that hierarchy." Both Davis and Dubberly encourage consideration of visual mapping issues such as shape, scale, proximity, and color to further emphasize conceptual relationships. For visual thinkers, the addition of these elements creates a more robust visual language.

Examining the results

Students and teachers can initially go over concept maps together to see how particular concepts were developed. The maps may need to be redrawn to clarify relationships, and subsequent maps can be developed as new information is gathered. Finally, concept maps are excellent as an initial wayfinding tool, in understanding and analyzing complex information. They provide an excellent jumping-off point for subsequent writing (freewriting, short essays) and sketching.

"...freewriting doesn't just get words on paper,

it improves things"

Peter Elbow, author and professor

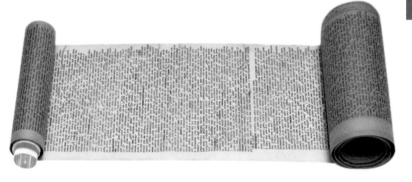

FREEWRITING

Jack Kerouac, the famous Beat Generation author, could be thought of as the quintessential "freewriter," exemplified by his book *On the Road*. Originally typed on a 120-foot scroll of paper (video) so he wouldn't have to stop his train of thought to change paper,[6] his unedited, freewheeling writing captured the energy and spontaneity of his travels and has influenced generations.

Freewriting is an excellent way to get your thoughts down on paper. It can be used in the preliminary phase or throughout the course of a project. Freewriting helps bring hidden ideas into the visible world, which is what art and design are all about. Allowing your thoughts about a subject to flow on paper, without any judgment, promotes an energetic discovery process.

As the words come out of your head, let them flow without concentrating on the rules of writing. Pages of freewriting can reveal new ideas and connections that may not emerge if initially developed with a more critical evaluation. Consider it private writing, as it is not typically judged by others.

How freewriting works

Freewriting is similar to journal writing, but it focuses more on a specific idea or question. Peter Elbow, professor of English at the University of Massachusetts, Amherst, and author of numerous books on writing, explains that there are unfocused and focused forms of freewriting.[7] The unfocused version allows you to simply put words on paper in response to a general thought or feeling about a topic or problem. In a sense, this is similar to journaling, where thoughts are put down without much focus. This is a good way to write about anxieties and questions surrounding a project.

In contrast, in a focused freewrite you are addressing a specific question.

For example, if you are exploring a new brand concept for an existing company, you might ask a question such as "what does the existing logo represent?" You have most likely thought about the existing logo, and maybe even discussed it with your colleagues, but by quickly and intensively writing your thoughts down, you make these thoughts concrete. The words are then available for you to further reflect on.

Freewriting is a technique that can take some time to master. Sometimes those unseen connections can produce exciting ideas. There is the possibility of moving too far off the topic. But the point is to relax and write freely about the subject, to stimulate more productive thinking and writing.

Developing a freewrite

Set a time frame for the freewrite, perhaps 10–15 minutes, and simply write about your topic, without lifting your pen from the paper or your fingers from the keyboard. Don't pause to think too much when writing, just try to keep your thoughts flowing (even if your next thought is "I don't know what more to write"). Don't worry about spelling, or even if the writing makes sense, as this is primarily for you. Write what you know about a given topic, and write questions about what you don't know. This can generate further writing that leads to more ideas.

By the end of the process, you will most likely have made some new discoveries about your project. Continue formulating different questions or ideas until you have a collection to read and reflect on.

The following are ways freewriting can be used when working on a visual project:

» Write for 10–15 minutes about the problem or the subject in a more general way (for instance, why you chose this topic, what it is about)
» Write for 10 minutes about everything related to the subject or problem
» Write down three words important to the subject or problem and then write for 10–15 minutes about those three words
» Midway through a project, write down what you have done in terms of concept development and idea searching, and what more could be done
» Pose a specific question about the project and answer it

Looping: how it works

Looping, another freewriting technique, is useful as a way to direct the freewrite back into itself. Remember, these exercises are meant to get you to think and write quickly, without the worry of correct spelling and grammar. Looping back into the freewrite forces you to privately evaluate what you wrote.

After your initial 10–15 minute freewrite, go back and read it. Circle what you consider the most interesting or provocative thought, perhaps one that you would like to further develop. For your next freewrite, begin with that sentence and spend another 10–15 minutes writing. By looping back, you are able to delve deeper into the subject, while still maintaining a vigorous and spontaneous spirit of discovery.

Examining the results

What do you do with your freewrites? It makes sense to read over them and notate sentences or phrases that may help in developing ideas further. Often new insights into a problem will arise.

BRAINWRITING

Brainwriting is the written equivalent of traditional brainstorming. Typically, brainstorming methods are used to develop new ideas for a project. In both methods, a small group will gather to exchange ideas and reactions. However, although brainstorming is a great way to generate ideas quickly, it may leave quieter group members out of the discussion. Brainwriting, in contrast, not only takes advantage of the group energy that traditional brainstorming sessions bring, but it is also a way to include those who are less comfortable expressing themselves through speech.[8]

How brainwriting works

In brainwriting, all group members use writing to develop ideas. The collaborative nature of brainwriting is perfect for team projects.

Developing a brainwrite

It is necessary to create a basic template to be used by each group. A common formula to create the template is 6-3-5, which means 6 people in a group each write 3 ideas for 5 minutes and then the paper is passed on to the next person. Each idea should be written as a complete, concise sentence. A person could use previous ideas as a stimulus for thinking of new solutions. The total time for this brainwriting session should be about 30 minutes.

Examining the results

Once the form is completed, discuss resulting ideas within the group.

Problem:		
Idea 1	Idea 2	Idea 3

Using a format such as this can help guide you through a group brainwrite exercise. The CD in the back of the book has a chart for your use.

WORD LISTS

Lists are part of our lives—from shopping lists to to-do lists. Perhaps it is the simplicity of seeing words listed that appeals to us, especially when we are typically inundated with a barrage of information. The typical use of a list is to check off an item that has been completed, which gives us a sense of control and accomplishment. Yet listing can go beyond helping us figure out things that need to be completed and is a quick way to use words for idea generation.

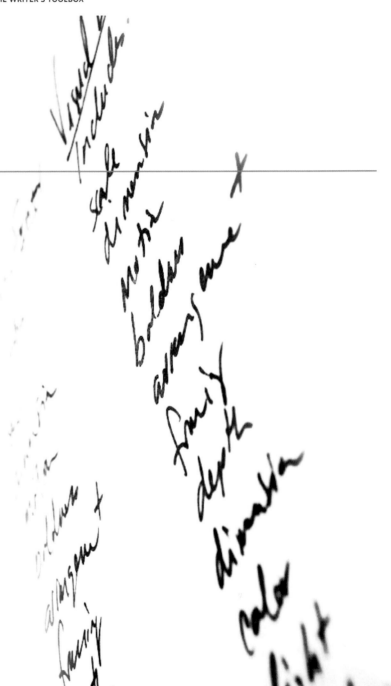

How word lists work

Much of what designers do is to distill a given problem down to its essential elements. Lists are concise, and the quickness in creating one allows a variety of associations to develop in a short time. Lists group words in distinct categories, and enable a divergency of ideas to occur.

Developing a word list

Start with a general concept word such as "light." Next, make a list of descriptive words, metaphoric words, or oppositional words, all relating to the word "light." Creating specific categories can help focus the list. The words that emerge can be used as a jumping-off point for further creativity exercises. Traditional writing tools, such as a dictionary and a thesaurus, can be useful. Thinkmap's Visual Thesaurus allows the user to see various relationships of words around a central hub.

Examining results

Once you have created several lists, look over them and circle words that stand out for one reason or another—perhaps the way they look, the way they sound, or what they mean. Continue exploring those words with other exercises to see where this leads.

Do you see a repetition emerging from these various ways of looking at the problem? Reflect on these repetitions and continue to delve deeper into the problem based on these new discoveries. The previous brainstorming exercises can help with idea generation for both written and visual projects. Outlines can help further shape and order ideas.

OUTLINES

Outlines are structures that help to organize information. A traditional outline defines content through headings and subheadings. It is basically a plan of, or guide to, ideas you want to address, making it easier to work on sections in any order. An outline acts as a framework to hold and organize ideas. For a piece of writing, it usually contains an introduction, a central idea, subsequent points backing up this idea, a summary, and a conclusion.

For a visual project, such as a book or a website, a storyboard or a series of small schematic sketches can act similarly to an outline, in showing the necessary content and order of the project.

"A writing plan is a mechanism for idea exploration and creative design"

Mike Sharples, author of How We Write: Writing as Creative Design

How an outline works

In some ways, the intent of an outline is similar to that of a typographic grid. Both are meant to give the author or the designer a structure for developing the piece. Whereas an outline uses headings and subheadings as a plan for main themes and detailed points to be covered, a typographic grid uses horizontal and vertical lines as guides for text and image placement.

Developing an outline

Sometimes you know more or less what you want to write and the order of topics you want to cover in a written piece. You may have done some initial research and thought about your topic, enough to be able to create a structured outline. Similarly, a designer may begin a project with a grid structure in place, based on the various elements (text and images) to be used in the piece. Yet sometimes it is difficult to know what points you want to make in a written document and the order you want to state them, or know what grid structure will work best for your piece.

Developing an outline following freewriting and brainstorming exercises creates a flexible way to move ideas around. For example, you might have created an idea matrix with sticky notes, categorizing certain ideas you might cover in the document. The sticky notes can be moved around and eventually shaped into a more concrete outline. To compare this to a typographic grid, a designer may first want to find the most dynamic composition by moving text and images on a page without a grid, and then impose a grid structure.

Examining the results

Whichever way you begin your project, it is important to keep flexibility in the process, by adding to, deleting from, and reordering the outline as necessary. Physically cutting and pasting an outline together can allow for a more tactile, visual result. To compare this to a typographic grid, it is important to know when to break out of the grid structure in order to create a stronger visual communication.

Multiple voices make a project stronger

WRITING AND CRITIQUES

Consider that no one knows more about your work than you do. You have made decisions in your process that have taken you to this point. But now you need a way to get your work to the next level. Having work evaluated and discussed is necessary to the creative process, and critiques provide the necessary forum.

How critiques work

Critiques allow for periodic input as you work through a project. The addition of many voices can make a piece stronger. The traditional format for critiques involves posting work on the wall, followed by discussions with colleagues or classmates. This type of critique can be tedious, as each person has to wait her turn for input. When writing is integrated into a critique, greater possibilities for energetic discussions emerge.

Developing critique strategies using writing

The following critique strategies use writing to reflect on in-progress and completed work. Though these examples are geared towards class situations, they can easily be adapted to projects and working situations outside of school.

Sticky notes
Once work is up on the wall, sticky notes are placed by the work according to three categories: "what is working," "what is not," "what next," if possible using three different colors. These notes are anonymous and can be written in the form of a question or a statement. The strength of this method is that it gives varied feedback and can provide a good starting point to talk further about work.

Feedback questions
Creators can direct the critique by bringing two or three questions regarding areas of their project in need of feedback. This can be conducted either with the entire team, in small groups, or one on one.

Peer review and response
Much like reflective writing, peer review and response can empower people to bring their work to the next level of development. In this situation, peers exchange work with one another and respond in writing to specific questions pertinent to their project. These questions can be generated by the participants or by a team leader.

Round-robin critique
A less formal method of bringing writing into a critique is through a kind of round-robin writing situation. Work is placed on a desk with a blank sheet of paper and a pencil or pen beside it. Participants then move from one desk to another, writing a brief comment about the work, based on specific criteria. These comments can be anonymous.

Voting
In this method, an entire group reviews all work. Individuals are asked to write a brief paragraph for the three pieces that best meet the project criteria. The written responses are used as a point of departure for further group discussion. As the discussion progresses, the pieces are ranked according to how they meet the project criteria.

(The following critique methods take advantage of web-based software. The advantage of web-based software is that users can upload media and utilize feedback any time. The observations made in critiques, both verbally and in writing, are critical to the creative process. A combination of these critique methods can help develop a stronger final piece.)

Flickr

The photo website Flickr is a great tool for viewing work online. Uploading images to Flickr is a quick way to share and receive comments by peers about work in progress.

Blogger

Google's free software allows the coordinator within minutes to set up a simple blog for posting comments. The templates are simple and well designed, and this software dovetails easily with Google's image storage software, Picasa.

Tumblr

Tumblr is another popular free blogging platform. With its customizability and effortless sharing, Tumblr is an inspiring site for designers and artists.

VoiceThread

This online tool is presented as a media album. Users are able to converse in any number of ways, from voicing comments and importing media, to doodling and annotating an idea in real time, so that others can see it.

REFLECTIVE WRITING

> *"Fill your paper with the breathings of your heart..."*
>
> *William Wordsworth*

Using brainstorm writing at the beginning of a project can generate innovative, lateral thinking. However, during the course of a project, or once it is completed, writing as a reflective tool can be extremely valuable.

How reflective writing works

Taking time to write reflections throughout the process allows for an in-depth analysis of the project, both on a micro and macro level. This may be as pragmatic as literally writing down everything you have accomplished on the project and everything you need to do to see it completed, such as details involving research, contacts, or deadlines. Alternatively, this reflective "in-process" writing can focus on pointed questions of a more general type. For example, at any given stage of a project, ask yourself: what was the learning experience for this project? Reflect on how you arrived at your concept. What makes it strong? How could you make it stronger? How did you arrive to the visual language of the project? What type of feedback has been helpful throughout the process? What has not? How might you have approached the project differently, knowing what you know at this time? These are just some of the questions that can be reflected on.

Developing reflective writing

As with freewriting, reflective writing is intended to be read only by you. It may be informally shared with your peers, but it is not a document that needs to be typed and edited. Sometimes it is helpful to do 10–15 minutes of reflective writing after a number of sketches have been generated. This would serve as a self-assessment or self-critique exercise. For example, you may be working on generating ideas for a logo. After an initial gathering of ideas, put your work up on a wall and reflect on the results in writing, before you begin a discussion with anyone else. Bring these written thoughts to the discussion or critique. Journals, sketchbooks, and blogs are great vehicles to document thoughts and reflections.

Examining the results

Reading over your reflections can help bring more insight to your subject. The reflections show how you have grown throughout your process, and what you have learned about yourself. The main thing is that these reflections get you to write, and that in turn will make you a better thinker, artist, and designer.

The most famous sketchbooks in history were created by Leonardo da Vinci (1452–1519). He filled countless sketchbooks with notes, diagrams, and drawings, exploring nature, art, and architecture. What was so amazing about da Vinci's sketchbooks? His sense of observation was keen, as his more than two hundred anatomical drawings attest. These notes and drawings enabled scientists and doctors to visualize and understand much more than was previously known about the human body. His handwritten notations illustrate his push to gain knowledge as well as the need to use both text and image to make discoveries.[9]

JOURNALS AND SKETCHBOOKS

Thomas Edison (1847–1931) was also a prodigious keeper of notebooks. His more than 3,500 notebooks, filled with ideas, diagrams, notes, and photos, were not discovered until after his death in 1931.[10] What makes Edison's notebooks impressive is how much of his creative process they reveal. He would go over the ideas and notes in his notebooks, which would then lead to new ideas.

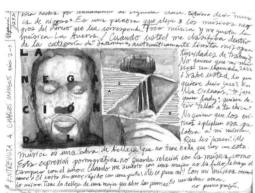

Sketchbooks: Julio Torres Lara

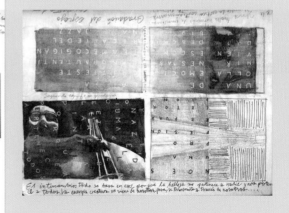

For example, his notes and diagrams on the transmission of sound...

THE TELEPHONE

...led him to think further about the recording of sound...

THE PHONOGRAPH

...which in turn led him to experimentation with recording images.[11]

MOTION PICTURES

(VIDEO)

How sketchbooks work

A sketchbook filled with your ideas, notes, and sketches on a day-to-day basis can strengthen your visual and writing acuity. A small journal or sketchbook can be easily carried around. Although the content of a sketchbook or journal is typically for your eyes only, you still get practice in putting your written ideas and visual thoughts onto paper. It is not so much what you say that is important, but the action of writing and drawing each day that strengthens your abilities. The more you do this, the more comfortable you will be in articulating your thoughts.

Developing a sketchbook

Find a sketchbook that will fit your needs and a pen that allows for a smooth flow of ideas and thoughts. Make a habit of carrying the book around with you, so that you get into a regular rhythm of thinking, writing, and sketching. Think of this book as a place to file your interests—what is it about the poster, the painting, the film you saw last night, the book you just finished, that has made you think more deeply and critically? Use freewriting to write down reactions to lectures, books, an article in a newspaper or magazine. Use the sketchbook to experiment with visual language—play with collage, painting, and drawing.

Designer and artist Julio Torres Lara uses his sketchbooks as a "personal diary in my evolution as an artist and designer." Torres develops rich sketchbooks for each of his projects, combining writing, drawing, and painting. He states, "It helps me in the same way as a compass helps a sailor out in the sea. It's my guide in the search for the solution to the problem. Besides helping me keep in touch with the organic process of design (drawing and writing), it saves time in my work."[12] Ideas and connections enter our awareness quickly and fleetingly, and sketching and writing help us capture this dynamic process.

Examining the results

Reviewing pages in your sketchbook can help you reflect on your ideas and creative process. An idea or sketch that didn't seem to work for one project may very well fit another. The beauty of a sketchbook is its physical nature—the tactile quality of turning pages filled with rich ideas is inspiring and can lead to better work.

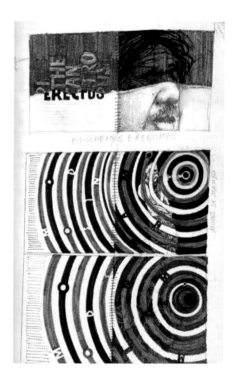

Sketchbooks: Julio Torres Lara

In sum, building confidence in writing is an ongoing process. It takes dedication, practice, and patience, and the more you write, the more confident you will become at expressing yourself in words. Whether alone or in tandem with sketching, writing helps organize and articulate ideas and manifest thoughts. Visual thinkers should utilize writing as another tool in their creative process. Adapt the exercises in this chapter as needed, and feel free to share new ideas on the Writing for Visual Thinkers website.

Take 20 minutes
Dedicate 20 minutes with nothing but a pen and paper in front of you (no computer). You can doodle, write short notes, etc. See what happens.

Experience poetry
Poetry, and in particular haiku, a form of Japanese poetry, can be a great vehicle for visual thinkers to write down succinct visual impressions. Pick up a poetry book at your local bookstore, or take a poetry class. A great way to hear a poem a day is to listen to *The Writer's Almanac*, with Garrison Keillor.

Take a closer look
Think about what movie, book, music you've always loved. For example, this could be a movie you've seen over and over. Why do you continue to re-watch this movie? Do you put it on just to have it play in the background as you do housework? Write one page quickly and intuitively: what is grotesque about it, or precious, or why is it a guilty pleasure for you?

New connections: mind map
Find an article. Circle five words in that article. Now come up with 10 words that could be associated in any way with those five words. Write a short narrative story threading all of these words together.

THINKING IN WORDS AND PICTURES 2

As visual thinkers, we think in words and pictures. When we work on creative problems, we write and sketch utilizing both sides of our brains. Words and pictures underlie the work of artists and designers. Understanding how words and pictures are processed and accessed can strengthen the creative process.

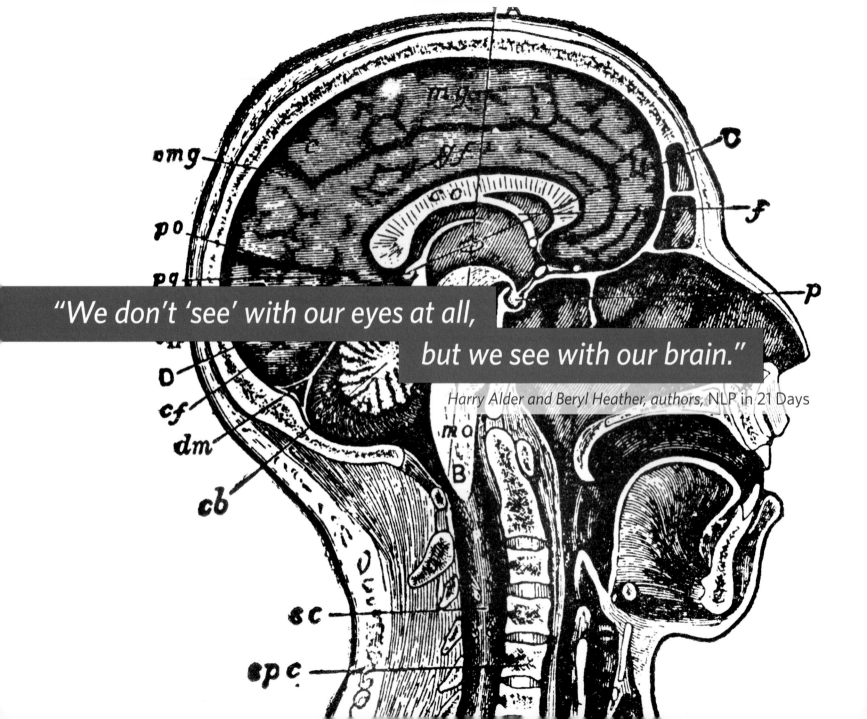

"We don't 'see' with our eyes at all,
but we see with our brain."

Harry Alder and Beryl Heather, authors, NLP in 21 Days

HOW THE BRAIN WORKS

The brain is the center of our being. This control center is vital to everything we do, from breathing to talking. Why would a book about the relationship between writing, art, and design contain a chapter on the brain? In order to understand how visual thinkers use their brain in writing, learning, and creativity, it seems useful to have a general understanding of its function.

It is commonly understood that the brain is composed of two sides: the left and right hemispheres. Although they look alike, they are considered "asymmetrical" because their cognitive functioning is very different. In fact, human beings are one of the few species with an "asymmetrical" brain.[1]

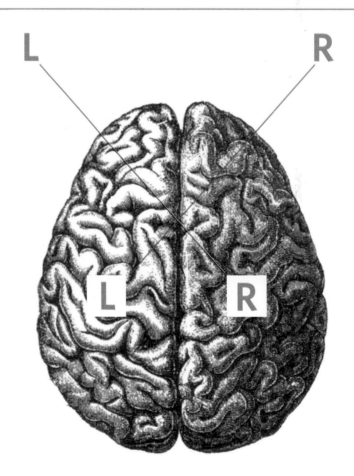

Neuropsychology

Much of what we know about how the brain functions in relation to human cognitive abilities is the
result of research done by specialists called neuro-
psychologists. One of the most famous was Nobel
Prize winner Roger Sperry, noted for his work with
split-brain patients. His subsequent experiments laid
the groundwork for better understanding of how
the two sides of an intact brain work independently
and in tandem with one another.[2]

It was long known that for sensory and motor purposes,
the left side of the brain controls the right side of the
body and vice versa. Thanks to Sperry's contribu-
tions, we now also know that the two hemispheres
work together with one another, each half contributing
with its own particular abilities.

Although the left and right hemispheres of the brain
have different strengths, there is no scientific proof
that one brain hemisphere or the other dominates
in an individual. Popular culture claims to be able to
train someone to be stronger in left-hemisphere or
right-hemisphere skills, but the truth is that we all
use both hemispheres continuously, switching back
and forth or combining skills from each to approach
various tasks. When those activities include language,
logic, computation, detail, analysis, and sequencing,
the left hemisphere is more active. In contrast, when
a more holistic, intuitive overview is needed, the
right hemisphere takes the lead.

Nevertheless, it is not the task that determines
which side of the brain is involved, but rather how
one approaches that task. Let's use a simple memory
game as an example. Say you have 20 cards with
different colors and patterns on them and you are
trying to match pairs of cards. Take a look at the
cards for a few minutes and then turn them over.

You could approach this task purely from a visuo-
spatial (right hemisphere) approach, trying to
remember which card had a particular pattern and
where it was located in the array. Alternatively, you
could approach the same task from a more verbal
(left hemisphere), analytical point of view, such as
subvocalizing "the second card on the left and the
third card from the bottom both have a blue design."[3]

Artists and designers can explore visual projects
with global, imagistic views (right-side), or as logical,
detailed sequences (left-side). We use language and
writing in our work, but we also have a keen awareness and understanding of space and the relationships of parts to the whole. So, to say that artists
and designers are right-brain oriented discounts the
"whole brain" approach necessary for optimal performance with any project.

In 1967, Sperry and fellow Caltech researcher Ronald Myers began experimenting with splitting the fibers of the corpus callosum, the thick bundle of millions of nerve fibers that connect the two hemispheres together. Sperry's split-brain procedure was performed on people with severe epilepsy. The result of the operation was a complete end to the seizures, but an additional result was the ability to observe the specific cognitive functions carried out by each hemisphere. Prior to the split-brain operation, it was thought that the two halves of the brain had interchangeable functions. Sperry's research and subsequent experiments (video) showed that in fact the two hemispheres hold specific cognitive functions.

Learning dynamics

Clearly, a person's particular approach to problem solving plays a large role in how they learn. Unsurprisingly, visual learners and thinkers often follow a visual, auditory, and kinesthetic learning style. This means that while some people learn best through reading and looking at pictures (visual), others need to hear words spoken (auditory), and others learn best by doing and making (kinesthetic). Often, visual thinkers use a combination of all three, depending on the task or project. But understanding your own personal learning style is only one part of the equation. How we think, communicate, and work also plays a role.[4]

Who are you?

An awareness of how you learn, think, work, and communicate can strengthen your abilities as an artist and designer. Understanding that there are many ways to approach a creative problem will make working collaboratively much easier. Apply your strengths, while understanding others' differences.

Learning styles
visual /auditory/kinesthetic

You prefer reading the novel (with illustrations), your friend prefers the book on tape.

You listen to a lecture about 3-D optics and your friend prefers to make a pair of 3-D glasses.

Thinking styles
internal/external visionary/detailed

You talk out loud about your ideas and your friend barely talks while working.

You like to look at the whole project, while your friend focuses on step-by-step details.

reading
pictures-images
demonstration
observation of others
body language
VISUAL

SYNESTHESIC
LEARNING STYLE

AUDITORY
speaking-lectures
listening-conversation

TACTILE/KINESTHETIC
doing-making
need activity to learn

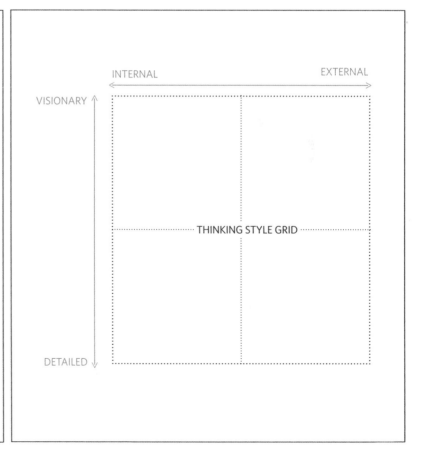

INTERNAL   EXTERNAL

VISIONARY

THINKING STYLE GRID

DETAILED

Communication styles
indirect/direct

You are working with others on a collaborative project and you find it hard to answer questions directly—in contrast, two group members easily verbalize their opinions and needs. Words flow off their tongues.

Working styles
alone/quiet/focused/shared/high energy/dynamic

You prefer to work alone in your studio, while your friend prefers working with others.

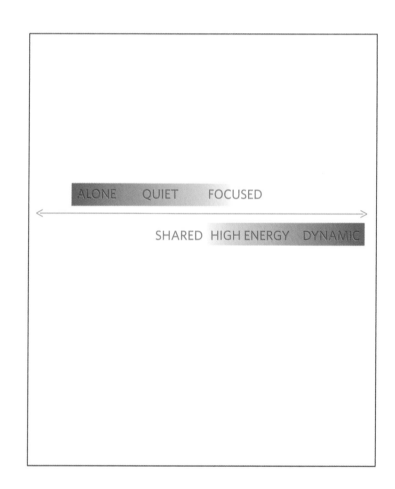

Stages of problem-solving

In the book *The Universal Traveler*, authors Don Koberg and Jim Bagnall outline seven "universal stages of creative problem-solving." Regardless of individual differences in communication/working/ thinking/learning styles, these "universal" problem-solving strategies can be applied to many types of projects and disciplines. Many of these stages include writing.

Accept situation (Commitment)

"Agreeing to direct sufficient energies toward resolving a particular problem, situation or goal; maintaining the necessary momentum to complete the task."

In the words of Charles and Ray Eames, "Design is constraints." Work with the problem at hand rather than lamenting over what could be if you could do whatever you felt like.

Analyze (Research)

"Gathering sufficient specific and general information to deal effectively with the situation; organizing the pertinent facts and feelings involved for developing a more complete and detailed view."

When the word "research" is brought up, there is often a sense that you will be sitting for hours in the library, sifting through books and journals: not necessarily so! In fact, analysis and research take on many forms. A creative research process can involve intuition, writing, speaking, listening, collecting, sketching, brainstorming, and collaborating. It can involve fieldwork, studio work, cross-disciplinary work, and ethnographic work.

As designer Bruce Mau states in his Incomplete Manifesto for Growth, "Process is more important than outcome. When the outcome drives the process we will only ever go to where we've already been. If process drives outcome we may not know where we're going, but we will know we want to be there."[6]

Remember that the more creative you are as a researcher, the richer the material you will have to work with and ultimately the stronger the project will be.

Define (Destination-finding)

"Identifying the key issue or issues; determination of primary cause or essence of the problem situation; translating negative problem conditions into viewpoints and/or objectives."

One of the best methods of defining a problem is writing a project summary or brief. A brief is a written explanation of the project, and is intended to aid in clarifying the project's goals and mapping out the project's approach. In graphic design, the project brief aids both the designer and the client. The brief can be written in narrative form; in a more condensed, bulleted format; or a combination of both.

Ideate (Shopping for options)

"Finding many possible alternative plans or ways for achieving the stated objectives or realizing the stated intentions."

This phase is often the most creatively energetic. Utilize lateral thinking strategies and brainstorming to develop many divergent solutions. It is often the phase when strong collaborative efforts can yield many ideas. Ideas at this phase are often written down and sketched. If working with a group, large sheets of paper can be spread out on tables or pinned to the wall to help facilitate concept mapping, diagramming, and writing.

Select (Decision-making)

"Choosing the way; selecting the 'best bet' from the menu of options generated; comparing alternatives with objectives to find an appropriate fit; determining a plan of action."

Here, you examine all of the possible ideas you and your team have come up with and you begin to converge on the best solutions. This phase allows the assessment of all ideas, with the stronger ones moving ahead to be further developed. Clients work collaboratively on finding the strongest solution.

Implement (Taking action)

"Putting the plan into operation; translating intentions into physical action or form; realization of the expectation or 'dream'".

Though you have undoubtedly spent time sketching and writing down ideas, this stage is where the visualization or prototyping of one or more ideas is fleshed out and becomes more concrete. Client and peer feedback shapes the concept, and it becomes clearer and more detailed.

Evaluate (Assessment)

"Review of process (means) as compared with products (ends) to determine worth of value received; making plans for future improvement."

Once the project is completed it is helpful to look back on the experience and write an assessment of both the process (means) and the final result (ends). In the industry it's called a "post-mortem," and whether it's done on problem projects or all projects, it's helpful in identifying what worked and what didn't and how future projects can run more smoothly. Assessing the project methodically allows for both personal and group improvement.

Possible questions you might ask yourself in assessing any project:

Process (Means)

» How was the process in developing this project?
» Was there enough communication?
» What new discoveries were made?
» Was there enough divergency in initial ideas?
» How was writing used to facilitate the process?

Project (Ends)

» How well did the project conceptually work out?
» How well did the project work formally?
» Did the project achieve its goal in reaching the target audience? How?
» How was writing used within the project?
» What would you change?

Case Study: IDEO

Let's look at a project the innovative product development firm IDEO worked on for a segment of a 1999 *Nightline* show titled "The Deep Dive." The project—to develop a new and innovative shopping cart in just 4 days—shows how these universal problem-solving practices can be put to work.

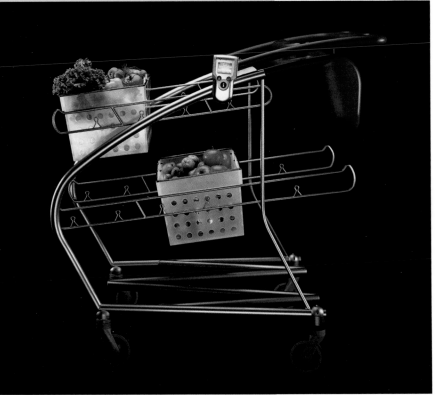

© IDEO

The multi-disciplinary team approach that IDEO is famous for—bringing together industrial designers, human factor specialists, interaction designers and mechanical engineers—allows for a "deep dive" to search for a unique solution. After the initial meeting, where CEO Dave Kelley explained the problem, teams began observing how people use shopping carts in stores—taking notes, taking photographs, and talking to people. Following this field research, teams analyzed their findings and brainstormed to find solutions.

Designers and engineers worked together to build a finished prototype to obtain user feedback. The result was an unique and flexible shopping cart that allows shoppers to scan their own items and drop them into removable plastic bins. A unique feature to the cart is the back wheels that turn both sideways and straight for easy maneuverability. Firms like IDEO are successful in large part due to the way they nurture the process of creativity. IDEO's collaborative approach to problems, coupled with a healthy dose of play, is what makes the firm one of the top five most innovative companies in the world.[7]

(The seven stages can systematically move you through a problem-solving task, but you may feel it's too restrictive, or that the problem you are working on demands that you approach it differently. *The Universal Traveler* points out five alternative pathways you can use:)

Linear process

Step-by-step logical sequence; being cautious of not getting ahead of yourself. Well-suited to large, complex, team projects.

Circular process

Starting at any stage and advancing to the others in turn. Ideal for lengthy projects.

Feedback approach

Moving forward while looping back to reconsider previous discoveries. Important when caution is imperative.

Branching paths

Allowing specific events and the interrelation of separate stages to control progress.

The natural pathway

Awareness of all stages concurrently, but emphasis on one or two steps at a time; like viewing seven open boxes in a row, each one ready to receive additional data and thereby modifying your overall thinking accordingly.[8]

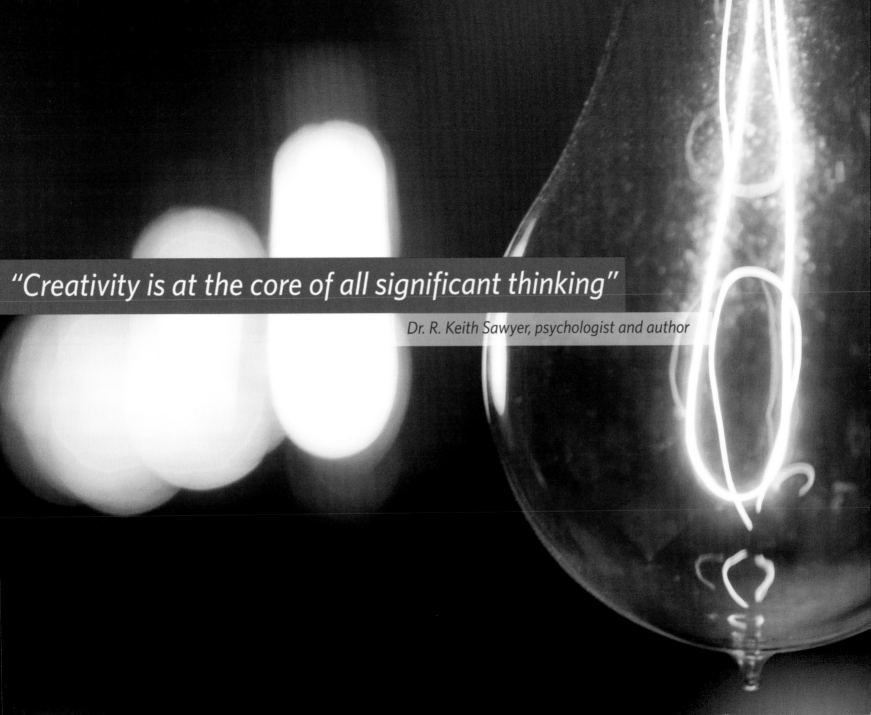

"Creativity is at the core of all significant thinking"

Dr. R. Keith Sawyer, psychologist and author

CREATIVITY

Although much neuropsychological research has been done in the realm of language, memory, and other cognitive functions and the brain, it has been much more challenging to explain how creativity is organized in the brain. One of the challenges neuro-psychologists face is finding the "center" of creativity (if there is one). This is due in large part to the fact that creativity draws from many connections made across different areas of the brain.

Another problem is pinpointing the moment when the brain is being creative. Though you may have an "aha" moment—that second when the problem at hand seems eminently clear—it is likely that the process of coming to that moment has been ongoing for a while. A great artist or scientist cultivates her work and findings for far longer than that "aha" moment leads us to believe. This is what makes the study of creativity and its relation to the brain so challenging.

In spite of the challenges, much has been researched and written about creativity and critical thinking. According to Keith Sawyer, professor of psychology and education at Washington University, and author of the book *Explaining Creativity: The Science of Human Innovation*, "Many people believe creativity comes in a sudden moment of insight and that this 'magical' burst of an idea is a different mental process from our everyday thinking. But extensive research has shown that when you're creative, your brain is using the same mental building blocks you use every day—like when you figure out a way around a traffic jam."[9]

Typically, creativity is a positive attribute given to an individual who looks at a problem in a new and different way. However, what may appear creative and innovative to one person—for example, a piece of music by John Cage—may seem silly and discordant to another. Happily, history has provided us with a long list of no longer controversial individuals who are considered brilliant in their creative endeavors. Scientists such as Galileo and Curie; artists such as Picasso and Magritte; musicians such as Debussy and Mozart; filmmakers such as Fellini and Hitchcock; and writers such as Hemingway and Emerson, are a sampling of the diverse areas where individuals have pushed creative boundaries.

One characteristic that seems to connect all great artists, scientists, and thinkers is the ability to explore a problem from many different angles and for as long as it takes—in some cases many years. "All the research shows that the creative process is basically the same: generating ideas, evaluating them and executing them, with many creative sparks over time," states Dr. Sawyer.

One of the leaders in the area of creative thinking and "thinking tools" is Edward De Bono. His lateral thinking technique has been used by a broad cross-section of people, from businesspeople and scientists to artists and designers. The basic assumption with lateral thinking is that it is better to think obliquely when generating ideas, than come at the problem with a narrower mindset. De Bono states that "the natural inclination is to search for alternatives in order to find the best one. In lateral thinking, however, the purpose of the search is to loosen up rigid patterns and to provoke new patterns." Discovering unrelated connections could in fact spawn a unique creative solution.[10]

Therefore, one way to interpret these ideas is to conclude that the creative process is much like a problem-solving task: complex and time consuming. Spontaneous, creative solutions, such as the apple that allowed Newton to conceive of gravity, are rare.

But the power of that vision has perpetuated a myth about how creativity evolves. Rather, creativity should be conceived of as a build-up process of creation and criticality interwoven throughout a given time period, and rather than a solo effort it's often the product of working in collaboration with others. This collaboration may be in formal groups, or it can emerge from informal conversations that give you new insights into the project.

One of the ways to grow and evolve as an artist and designer is by being aware of how you learn, think, communicate, and work. Artists and designers happen to do this with words and pictures. Understanding the basic structure of how the brain informs the creative mind can lead to a stronger and more innovative process, which in turn will lead to more exciting work.

Flip the medium
Look at a piece of work by a well-known artist or designer and think about how that work would translate to another medium. Write a paragraph describing in detail how the new piece would look. Do this same exercise with one of your own pieces of art or design.

Go to a familiar place
Go to a familiar place and experience the place with a new sense. For example, go to your favorite coffee shop and close your eyes and listen to the sounds and conversations for 10 minutes. How do your other senses come into play? What do you notice about the physical space? What smells permeate the space? Write down your observations.

Make a process book
A process book enables you to see where you began and where you are going. It should be a gathering of materials that assist you in your process (quotes, images, freewrites, good ideas/bad ideas, research).

Document your next creative project (even a non-visual project such as a book of poems) with a process book. The book can be a simple binder.

Create a DADA grab bag
The DADA artists used random words and images to create powerful art. Their process was as simple as putting words or images from a newspaper into a bag, shaking it, and dumping the contents onto a table. This was then a jumping off point for other creative projects, such as collage, poetry, sculpture, and experimental music.

In this vein, take a magazine or newspaper and cut out roughly 20 images and words. Place them in a bag, shake it, and reach in and grab one of the pieces. Based on the image or word, begin writing a 50-word narrative that has a beginning, middle, and end. Write quickly and imaginatively.

Find the metaphor
A metaphor uses one concept to describe another. Creating metaphors is a great way to push yourself to think less literally. For example, find aspects of an animal that represents aspects of you (how you look, how you act, how others see you, or an experience you have had). Think about how you can incorporate metaphors into your art or design projects.

VERBAL AND VISUAL CONNECTIONS

3

The 21st century is a visual time, in which words and images share a close connection. Add a profusion of technology into this relationship and you will find new ways to think about the term "literacy." The bottom line is that traditional notions of reading and writing have changed, and this has opened up new opportunities for artists and designers to think about reading, writing, and publishing in our visual culture.

VERBAL LITERACY

"Literacy" (1883): the quality of being literate
(able to read and write) — Merriam-Webster Online

We all know that literacy is the ability to read and write, and it's something most of us take for granted. We learn at an early age how abstract symbols (letters) string together to form words and represent thoughts. We read and write for pleasure, for inspiration, for work, and for understanding. More than ever, language extends beyond words, as icons and images commingle with text. We live in an age where chatting on your computer, browsing the Internet, and texting on your phone happen at the same time. This multi-tasking between reading and writing multiple content types is the fractured way that much of our media is digested. This is not necessarily a bad thing, but it does have an impact on how we access and evaluate information. It also affects those who format writing for different kinds of consumption, such as artists and designers.

Visual literacy

"Visual Literacy" (1973): the ability to recognize and understand ideas conveyed through visible actions or images (as pictures)—Merriam-Webster Online

Visual literacy refers to an understanding of how to create and use imagery, as well as an awareness of how a particular image delivers a message. Artists and designers are required to have fluency and proficiency with visual elements—to be visually literate—in their work. But it is no longer the sole province of the visual communicator. Today's digital media provides endless combinations of words and images. Moreover, modern software makes the creation and manipulation of images easy. Now everyone—not just designers and artists—must be visually literate. Because artists and designers have a distinct advantage in our image-rich culture, we also have an obligation to teach others about the importance of visual literacy.

Like traditional linguistic literacy, visual literacy skills can be learned. Textbooks such as *Writing in a Visual Age*, *Beyond Words*, and *Picturing Texts* are being used in college-level communication and humanities courses to aid students in understanding the power of word-image relationships. These courses teach the value of considering visual images and text as a hybrid language.

Both writing and visual work involve the notion of context. Context refers to the aggregation of all the elements not actually in the work that affect the reading of it, such as the mores of the time when it was made. For example, the word "nigger" is shocking now, but it wasn't when Mark Twain wrote *The Adventures of Tom Sawyer*. The textbook *Picturing Texts* defines two distinct perspectives to consider when reading texts (text here referring to both words and images). The first is by asking, what is the immediate context in which the text is being read? This has to do specifically with the author, subject, and audience.[1]

Some questions you might consider within the realm of the immediate context are:

» Who created the piece and for what, audience?
» Who commissioned the piece?
» In what context is the image or piece going to be viewed?

The second thing to consider is the broader context: the social, historical, economic and cultural influences that may affect the meaning of the text.

Some questions you might consider within the realm of the broader context are:

» What does the piece say about our society?
» Our history?
» An event?
» Our identity and culture?

Seeing these connections can help visual thinkers approach writing and language from a more familiar perspective.

Critical and creative thinking

Why do we hate the word "critical"? Perhaps the phrase "reading critically" conjures up hours spent in front of dense academic papers, trying to interpret and analyze obscure language. Or maybe the word "critique" makes you think you must find fault with everything the author states. Yet our teachers keep making us write critiques... are we missing something?

Let's begin by defining the word "critical" in the context of critical thinking. Merriam-Webster's online dictionary defines it as exercising or involving careful judgment or judicious evaluation."[2] That doesn't sound too bad.

Moreover, the Thinker's Guide series publication *Critical and Creative Thinking* states, "To read well, one must actively construct an interpretation, imagine alternative meanings, imagine possible objections and thus think creatively while reading. Beyond that, one has to assess and judge... when one reads. Reading is not good reading—accurate, clear, plausible—unless it is also critical reading."[3] Of course, you don't approach everything you read the same way: a textbook is read differently from a novel or a magazine. What's important is that you develop an understanding of how critical thinking can be applied to gain understanding of what you read, and ultimately to become better at communicating in both words and pictures.

Despite the fact that our fast-paced, multi-tasking culture leaves little spare time, reading critically—reading with focus and concentration—is worth making time for. It does not mean you must be "overly-critical" and challenge everything being said, but it also does not mean you need to agree with the author's ideas. By evaluating what is being said (against what you know), interpreting what is being said, and constructing new meanings and interpretations, you can formulate a personal point of view about the text that allows you a richer comprehension of the author's meaning. You may even find that your own understanding of the world becomes more nuanced, and reading becomes more rewarding.

Here's how:
Read an article at least twice for meaning: the first time for macro comprehension—in essence, looking at the broader message being said—and the second time for better comprehension of micro ideas.

When reading printed articles, make visual notations in the margins and highlight passages to help clarify what is being said. If the article has notes or a bibliography, use those to further your research.

When reading articles electronically, you may not want to print everything out. Google Bookmarks and Diigo are just two free applications for keeping track of online material. Google Bookmarks (one of many integrated online tools from search giant Google) lets you collect, label, and comment on bookmarks, and also collect them in lists to keep private or share with the public. Diigo, another free service, lets you add stickies and highlights to any web page, create lists for yourself or colleagues and collaborators, and share links through email, Facebook, or Twitter.

The beauty of the web is finding connections and relationships that make sense to what you are searching for. As you read, you are essentially acting as an editor and creating new narrative structures each time you click on a link. However, while the visual dynamism of the web is helpful for visual thinkers to see connections and relationships, be sure to focus on what you set out to evaluate. Clicking from one link to another is engrossing, and can easily lead you off track. Try to stay focused on the topic.

"The best way to learn good writing is to read good writing"

Ellen Lupton

Relationship of text and the visual: reading

Today, if you asked someone what they read, they would probably name five or six different types of media including:

» journals and magazines
» websites
» newspapers
» traditional print and online books
» e-mail
» instant messages
» blogs
» forums and group messages
» tablets
» e-readers

Much of this media involves visual components—images, diagrams, animation—as well as interactive elements such as hypertext links. The way in which we interact with text continues to evolve, which in turn changes the way we read.

We live in an abbreviated world—much of our information has been reduced to short snippets and sound bites. It's not that we don't read any more, it's that often what we read demands less attention and no critical thinking. IMing and chatting on Facebook and other social networking sites is pleasurable and obviously involves reading and writing, but how often do you see any writing longer than a few paragraphs? How are good old-fashioned printed books faring in this age of competing reading arenas? You might think nothing can replace the intimate, tactile quality of a book. Yet Amazon's ebook reader Kindle, which can download a book in 60 seconds or less from its catalog of over 650,000 books, has changed the way we think about reading. In January 2011, Amazon sales of ebooks surpassed sales of print versions of those books for the first time.[4] Though the physical quality of a plastic ebook reader may seem uninviting, the speed and availability of reading material provide enough convenience that adoption is growing at an incredible rate. The Apple iPad's full color display and interactivity make it a unique reading platform for now, but many similar devices are on the horizon or already here.

An insightful article titled "Scan This Book" offers a glimpse into the future of the book as we know it. The author, Kevin Kelly, founding executive editor at *Wired Magazine* and author of several books, including *Out of Control: The New Biology of Machines, Social Systems and the Economic World,* and his most recent book, *What Technology Wants,* claims that in the very near future, the Universal Library will house millions of digitized books and change the way the world reads and accesses information. He states, "Despite the opposition of publishers and their lawyers, the world's texts are being electronically copied, digitized, searched and linked... and everything we thought we knew about books is going to change."[5] The future of the book is both exciting and mind-boggling.

According to Kelly, "turning inked letters into electronic dots that can be read on a screen is simply the first essential step in creating this new library. The real magic will come in the second act, as each word in each book is cross-linked, clustered, cited, extracted, indexed, analyzed, annotated, remixed, reassembled and woven deeper into the culture than ever before."[6] Think about how revolutionary the World Wide Web was in 1993, when it was first introduced to the public. Within a short time, much of the world became a "linked" entity. The digital library will play an equally important role in connecting ideas and voices.

Kelly points out that those who will benefit the most from the Universal Library are not those of us who have readily available libraries and bookstores. Rather, it is "the underbooked—students in Mali, scientists in Kazakhstan, elderly people in Peru— whose lives will be transformed when even the simplest unadorned version of the universal library is placed in their hands."[7] Though traditional print material has its tactile appeal, digital reading offers unique benefits of portability and easy access. But what is the effect on you as an artist or designer?

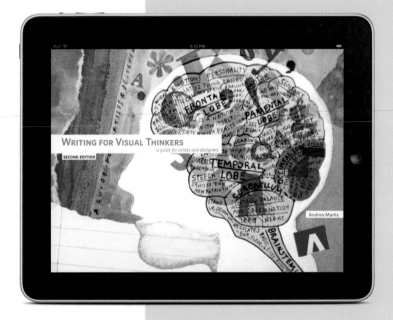

As digital media (such as blogs, podcasts, video, and animation) open up new possibilities for communication, it is hard to say where 21st-century literacy is headed. Artists and designers are now reaching audiences who possess more visual literacy, and this creates new and exciting challenges for both creator and audience. Our digital culture offers opportunities like never before, and visual thinkers are in a prime position to help shape ideas of literacy for the 21st century.

Write a review of a TED Talk (TED.com)
The TED talks are successful because they have a very simple formula: Have someone talk about something they are passionate about for 18 minutes. Some of the speakers use visuals and some don't. Write a description of one of the TED talks using 18 words. Write a review of one of the TED talks using 18 well-crafted sentences.

Animate your writing
Try to animate a word, a sentence or a paragraph. How do motion and sound affect the meaning of your words? For this exercise you would need a basic knowledge of AfterEffects, Flash, or Final Cut Pro.

Take the time
In a world where there is so much visual stimulation, take an hour off and simply listen to a story being told. Download a podcast from *Radiolab* or *This American Life* (or tune in on your public radio station). Both of these shows are rest for the eyes and a treat for the imagination. Close your eyes, listen to the podcast, and think about the visuals from the show. Write down your thoughts and observations, then record them and listen to your recording.

Pass it on
Write the first paragraph of a story and illustrate that paragraph in some way, then pass that to someone else to let them continue the story. As the piece continues to be passed, each subsequent writer only sees the previous paragraph. Try this as both a print book and an electronic book.

Take a walk
With a portable recorder, take a walk as long or as short as you want, and describe all that you are experiencing. Transcribe your recording into words and create a visual piece from this.

Narrative Structures:
Verbal and Visual Working Together

4

How does the word "narrative" relate to both written and visual work? Narrative structures are embedded in a story to help give the story a framework. Narrative moves a person through a story in a pleasurable and compelling fashion. A narrative can be heard, as in a radio play; it can be watched, as in a film; it can be read, as in a novel; it can be danced to, as in a song; and even seen/read, as in a graphic novel. Narrative structures vary depending on the medium and the purpose. A traditional linear narrative structure typically depends on a page-to-page reading for comprehension. A nonlinear narrative allows for the reader to move independently throughout a piece, often creating new meanings from discovering connections. But they all share one important and all so human job: to tell us a story.

STORYTELLING

Storytelling is a core human experience. Stories help us see how others view the world and help us find meaning in our lives. They help us grieve, help us celebrate, console us, and reinvent us. They are used in school to teach, in business to improve work habits, and in entertainment to escape. Stories are the difference between pain and pleasure in any communication activity.

Storytelling began as an oral tradition, combining speech with gestures, expressions, and sometimes music to help storytellers remember the narrative. With the development of writing, stories could be not only documented and preserved, but further enriched with illustrations. Finding intersections in your visual and verbal work can strengthen both. Think of your next visual project as a story to be told.

Jakob Trollbäck, president and creative director of Trollbäck + Company, talks about his storytelling approach to visual problem solving in his article "One Designer Shares: How to Use Design to Tell a Story." Trollbäck combines writing narratives and sketching in his process, whether creating a new company brand or an animation. He views "design as a language and as a way to communicate," and begins many projects by picking up a pen and writing a script.

The script can help organize thoughts and reveal "the essence of your approach." He asks questions such as "what's the idea and philosophy of the approach?" The script helps determine the premise of the story, or as Trollbäck refers to it, the "plot" of the story. Next, he looks at adding the necessary elements to help give the story its richness. He calls this "setting the scene." His list of places to find inspiration for these elements includes poems, movies, architecture, music, dance, anything that moves him. Trollbäck will often create a project for one medium, say, film, and then re-create the same story in another medium like print. This allows him to see how the message or story holds up.[1]

Approaching a visual project from a storytelling perspective can bring a unique richness to the final message. The following examples show how narrative structures appear in various media.

Slide shows

When we think of slide software, we usually think about the countless slide presentations we have sat through with too much bulleted text, too many incomprehensible graphs, combined with clip art in a color that is difficult to read. In the hands of one who understands visual narrative, a PowerPoint (or Keynote) presentation can turbocharge a message. A picture is worth a thousand words. Some caveats apply, though...

According to Edward Tufte, (video) slideware such as PowerPoint has forced a profusion of bad content upon unknowing and innocent audiences. In the article titled "PowerPoint is Evil," he states, "Rather than learning to write a report using sentences, children are being taught how to formulate client pitches and infomercials. Elementary school PowerPoint exercises (as seen in teacher guides and in student work posted on the Internet) typically consist of 10 to 20 words and a piece of clip art on each slide in a presentation of three to six slides—a total of perhaps 80 words (15 seconds of silent reading) for a week of work."[2] Tufte, author of the award-winning books *The Visual Display of Quantitative Information, Envisioning Information, Visual Explanations*, and his latest book, *Beautiful Evidence*, is a master at revealing how complex information (text and images) can in fact be both beautiful and meaningful. His argument is that software such as PowerPoint, when used without an understanding of narrative structures, image use, and typography, encourages presenters to create short, bulleted info bites, often at the cost of the content itself.

Fortunately, artists and designers are in a position to create both beautiful and meaningful electronic narrative presentations. As visual thinkers, their understanding of both the formal and theoretical framework of narrative structure puts them in a unique position to create powerful slide shows that make sense. Understanding text/image relationships (what is stated and how it looks) is key to helping an audience see the power in a visual narrative.

The musician and artist David Byrne (video) has been using PowerPoint as an art medium for several years. Byrne defends the software as "more than just a business tool—as a medium for art and theater."[3] His book *E.E.E.I. (Envisioning Emotional Epistemological Information)* is a collection of images and essays packaged with a DVD of five of his visual/audio PowerPoint presentations. Byrne took advantage of what the software had to offer (automatic slide shows, simple transitions, symbols) and combined these with his own photographs and music. As Byrne notes, "Although I began by making fun of the medium, I soon realized I could actually create things that were beautiful. I could bend the program to my own whim and use it as an artistic agent."[4]

Think of a slide show like any multiple-page document. The slide show "Death by PowerPoint" does a great job of illustrating the dos and don'ts of slide presentations. There should be a clear introduction to the topic, supporting points, and a summary ending. Take advantage of what the medium has to offer (a simple but effective narrative structure, ease of combining words and images) and build a compelling story. Never forget that there is a person talking; remember the slide show is a complement to the script and shouldn't be the script.

Explore slideshare.net's slidecasts area for more examples of ways in which visual narratives are combined with audio podcasts. As well, a rich visual presentation such as Al Gore's documentary *An Inconvenient Truth* can help visual thinkers see relationships between the visual and the verbal. No matter what you think of his politics, the combination of verbal and visual in Gore's talk was compelling enough to both raise awareness of global warming and win the man a Nobel prize.

IMAGE / TEXT NOVELS

A typical novel is usually printed in black and white, with little to no imagery: think of paperbacks that smell like newsprint and contain pages of justified text. Yet more and more examples can be seen of novels, both fiction and nonfiction, that push the boundaries of text and images in unconventional ways.

The book *VAS: An Opera in Flatland* is a unique novel that offers a visually rich, hybrid narrative. Author Steve Tomasula and illustrator Stephen Farrell use an exquisite array of visual concepts to illustrate the unique storyline. Another novel that does this in a more subtle way is the book *Extremely Loud & Incredibly Close* by Jonathan Safran Foer. Throughout the novel, the author intersperses devices such as black-and-white photographs, video stills, typographic experiments, graphic elements, and even blank pages to emphasize the poignant narrative of a child's reality following 9/11.

Graphic designer, book artist, and performer Warren Lehrer is internationally known for his many books that incorporate text and imagery. These include *Versations, I Mean You Know, French Fries, Nicky D. from L.I.C., Crossing the BLVD: Strangers, Neighbors, Aliens in a New America*, and his latest book *The Rise and Fall of Bleu Mobley: a life in books.* Lehrer has been influential in crossing boundaries among words, design, art, and performance in both fictional and documentary narratives. His lectures are a combination of visual presentation and theater performance. As Lehrer says, "I'm interested in re-evaluating the rote way we tend to use language, the more pedestrian way we go about writing... I compose text and stories and when it is put into book form, I use typography as the vehicle to see that text realized so it becomes a composition."[5]

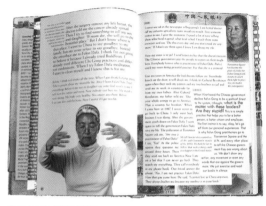

Crossing the BLVD, 2003

French Fries, 1984

Hypertext fiction

Non-traditional ways of reading, such as hypertext fiction, allow the reader to move through the narrative structure however they choose. Click on one link and you might end up rescuing people, but click on another link, you might fight in a battle. In essence, readers choose their own path in the narrative. An example of this in book form is the "Choose Your Own Adventure" series, in which the reader chooses a particular page and creates a new narrative.

Storyspace and HyperCard, two early hypertext programs, paved the way for more complex interactive environments. The use of hypermedia today extends far beyond these early programs, into stories, games, the Internet, art, and design. The hypertext fiction book *Grammatron*, by the artist and writer Mark Amerika, became a landmark cyber-novel and was one of the first pieces of Internet art to be accepted into the 2000 Whitney Biennial.[6]

Graphic novels / Comics

The term "graphic novel" typically refers to a comic-book-style story with an extended narrative, bound into a book form. This visual art form evolved from traditional comics, and over the past 10–15 years has become somewhat of a cult genre.

The graphic novel is a powerful visual storytelling medium, with its use of iconic visual language, hand-written type, and diverse sequencing of narratives. Graphic novels can help visual thinkers interpret and explore subject matter from historic to fantastical in new ways with few restrictions. They utilize literary devices such as symbolism, simile, allegory, and metaphor just as traditional books do, but their unique nature asks the reader to dig a little deeper into interpreting the story.

Image from graphic novel Wake the Devil, *of the Hellboy series by Mike Mignola.*

In 1969, the author John Updike (who was interested in becoming a cartoonist as a child) was giving a lecture addressing various new ways a novel might be presented. He stated: "I see no intrinsic reason why a doubly talented artist might not arise and create a comic strip novel masterpiece".[7]

While Updike's lone genius theory has been realized in such masterpieces like Art Spiegelman's *Maus*, more often graphic novels are group efforts, just as plays and films are. For example, the noir take on Batman, *The Long Halloween*, sports an almost film-length credit list: it's written by Jeph Loeb, drawn by Tim Sale, has colors by Gregory Wright, letters by Richard Starkings and Comicraft, and thanks the creator of Batman, Bob Kane.

While many are quick to write off comics as foolish escapism, a new breed of comics has emerged that tells powerful personal narratives. In Art Spiegelman's *Maus*, we see a child of Holocaust survivors come to understand both his parents' eccentricities and their nightmarish past, told visually with Jews portrayed as mice and Germans as cats.

This visualization doesn't soften the all-too-familiar stories of gas chambers and mass burial, but rather the use of familiar childhood symbols increases the dread and horror.

The simple drawings of Marjane Satrapi's *Persepolis* (video) allows us to place ourselves in the story of a rock-and-roll girl growing up in Iran during the Islamic revolution. Their abstract nature somehow allows us to relate to something alien to Western culture.

Even superheroes have grown up in modern graphic novels; Alan Moore's *Watchmen* (video) looks at psychosis as a source of "dressing up to fight crime" and represents it visually in Rorschach's ink-blot mask.

One of the best ways to learn about comics is to read the bestselling book *Understanding Comics: The Invisible Art* by Scott McCloud. In this over 200 page black- and-white comic book, McCloud cleverly illustrates and analyzes the history of narrative structures and how words and pictures work together to communicate ideas.

The following list of noteworthy graphic novels/comics reveals a wide variety of stories, from the more classic "superhero" genre (Watchmen and Dark Knight), to Sandman's straddling classical and comic mythology, to Maus's personal retelling of history.

Maus: A Survivor's Tale by Art Spiegelman (1992 Pulitzer Prize Winner)

Watchmen by Alan Moore and Dave Gibbons

The Dark Knight Returns by Frank Miller

Bone: One Volume Edition by Jeff Smith

The Sandman by Neil Gaiman

Palestine, Safe Area Goražde, The Fixer by Joe Sacco

Persepolis by Marjane Satrapi

American Born Chinese by Gene Luen Yang

Jimmy Corrigan: The Smartest Kid on Earth by Chris Ware (video)

Fun Home; a family tragicomic by Alison Bechdel

Understanding Comics by Scott McCloud

Zap Comix, Keep On Truckin' by R Crumb

American Splendor by Harvey Pekar

Hellboy by Mike Mignola

With so many exciting examples in our image/text-rich culture, now is a great time to explore narrative structures and how the visual and verbal work together. The interesting visual-verbal connections in presentations, illustrated novels, interactive stories, and highly visual graphic novels add richness to the ways we communicate. Working with a visual project as a narrative strengthens both your verbal and your visual thinking. So, think about your next project as a story and explore the many ways it can be told.

Internet narrative
The Internet is a perfect tool to explore a narrative structure.
Each time you click on a website or a link, you have created
a path or thread. Create a short written narrative based
on the last 10 links or sites you visited on the Internet. How
could you write a story based on the order of your exploration?

Look at a picture
Find an image with people in it and think about what they
see when they are looking outside the frame of the picture.
This forces you to write from a different point of view.

Making marks
Find an existing artifact that contains writing (for example,
an old phone book or a brown grocery bag) and make
marks (visual, words) over the existing text to create a new
visual piece.

Open the mystery drawer
Everyone has a drawer (usually in the kitchen) filled with
random objects such as keys, pennies, old batteries,
birthday candles, matchbooks, and tape. Determine the
order the objects seem to have been added to the drawer
and base a narrative on that.

Find five quotes
Find five quotes that inspire you about art or design. Next,
write a one-page story and insert these quotes within the
story, as part of the narrative. This can be a personal narrative, fiction, or a combination. Place quote marks around
the quotes, but it is not necessary to include who said the
quote within the story. (The citation can be place at the
very end of your story.)

Writing and Editing in the 21st Century

5

There is as much craft to good writing as there is in the craft of painting, drawing, or designing. The use of proper grammar and spelling is as essential as choosing the right brush, drawing medium, or appropriate typeface. The role of editing is crucial to the craft of any written work. Just as your visual work is vastly improved via interaction with a talented creative director, a skilled editor can raise your writing from blogfodder to *New Yorker*-quality prose. Approach writing as you would a visual project, with energetic critiquing and revising cycles, to strengthen your written work and assure it matches the quality of your design or art work.

Artist/Designer as editor

Designer and writer William Drenttel makes a good case for the state of design writing in his essay, "The Written Word: The Designer as Mediator." According to Drenttel, "designers frequently control the editorial content of their projects. They become, in effect, the editor, determining the 'story,' hiring the writer, assigning the artwork."[1] He points out that the visual shouldn't supercede the verbal in a design project and that designers have much to learn from the editorial world.

However, with the ease of digital technology, the role of editor is either overextended or nonexistent. From remixing music with GarageBand and creating playlists on iTunes to combining appropriated imagery remixed in Photoshop to publish on thousands of websites, people are able to create and edit media projects like never before. Yet, ability does not guarantee quality. The Internet has given rise to more and more unedited solo efforts while auteurs are as rare as they ever were. How do young creators find a place to hone their chops? Self-authored collaborative projects that explore topics and themes outside of commercial constraints are excellent ways to strengthen both your authoring and editing skills.

PDX Music Memory
Art Director: Joshua Berger
Designer: Linda Reynen
Editors: Jon Raymond,
Tiffany Lee Brown
Plazm magazine, issue #29

MUSIC MEMORY

'75   1980   1985   1990   1995   2000

PDX

CHOP SUEY
HUNG FAR LOW
COCK

THE CATS
IMPERIALIST PIGS
LUTEK
CLEAVERS
RUBBERS
EGMA
NEO BOYS
OILY BLOODMEN
Poison Idea
cloudz
KINETICS
DAN REED NETWORK
WIPERS
SADO-NATION
WATCHMEN
THE BOY ZOMBIES
NAPALM BEACH
Snow Bud and the Flower People (sideproject)
BILLY RANCHER AND THE UNREAL GODS

FINAL WARNING
THE JACKALS
PERFECT CIRCLE
MIRACLE WORKERS
BOY WONDERS
THEATRE OF SHEEP
STEVEN WRAY
MEAT HARSH
LOBDELL
BIG DADDY
HITTING BIRTH
RANCID VAT
THE HELL COWS NEVER OVER
SWEATY NIPPLES
CONCRETE JUNGLE
CRAZY 8s
GERN BLANSTON
PETE MISER
PLASTIC
AND THE FIVE FINGERS OF FUNK
HORN OF EVIL
DRUNK AT ABIS
GODS FAVORITE
PUSSY
MOTORGOAT (BECAME QUASI)
BUGSKULL
SONE
JARVIK 7 (BUGSKULL/SONE SPINOFF)

OBITUARIES
KILLING FIELD
INSANE JANE
DEAD MOON
SLACK
KURTZ PROJECT
BEDSPRING
RAW HEAD REX
FLEUR DE LYS
THE OBLIVION
RESIST
NU SHOOZ
NU-TELS
VENA RAYS
DHARMA BUMS
 king black acid
roger nusic
WORRIED GUYS
TRIO
HAZEL
AIRIAN
LOVEBUTT
M99
SPRINKLER
Pond
THIRTY OUGHT SIX
RED VIRUS
SEEKERS
APE
GRAVE
NEW BAD THINGS
BUSH HOG
MR. PHARMACIST
ANAL SOLVENT
SYNCOPATH
OLD TIME RELIJUN
GADGET
TOMMI STUBBS
GRAVES
REBECCA PEARCY
CALAMITY Jane
HEATMISER
THE DICKEL BROTHERS NO. 2
BEAM DRESCH
EVERCLEAR
SID MERRITT
THRILLHAMMER
CRACKERBASH
MIRKIN
PETE KREBS
pink martini
DR. HIGH
SISSYFACE
THE MULTNOMEN
GLASS CANDY
& THE SHATTERED THEATRE
LAND OF THE BLIND
SATAN'S PILGRIMS
JACKIE-O MOTHERFUCKER
Miranda July
TOPIARY
KINGS
GADGETTO
THE HELIO SEQUENCE
Sarah Dougher
SURF MAGGOTS
INDEX
THE MAROONS (FROM DHARMA BUMS)
31 KNOTS
SVELT
SOLENOID
DOPEY
MACHINE
ALL GIRL SUMMER FUN BAND
MIRAH
PANTHER
VALET
TALKDEMONIC
DRUNKEN PRAYER
ELLIOTT SMITH
THE DECEMBERISTS
THE SHINS
POOLSIDE
TRA LA LA
THE REARY
parenthetical girls
SPACE
BRAINWARMER
ZOE KEATING
IN THE RED
BLUES GOBLINS
POINT LINE PLANE
HUSTLER
MESMER
SLOW WHITE
LORIS
CHILDHOOD
FRIENDS
THE THERMALS
REPLIKANTS
THE GROADIES
STEPHEN MALKMUS & THE JICKS
DIABOLICAL CANDY
AUDITORY SCULPTURE
RECLINE
GRAPHIC
THE FEELINGS
GAME LEG
HARDON
TORSO
THE YO-NO'S
CARMINA PIRANHA SCARUM
A Nat Hema
THE STARLINGS
WESTERN & THE GROADIES
THE HAGGARD
THE WATERY
COUNTRYPOLITANS
SUFI MIND
THE STANDARD
STARPOWER
GOLDEN VOID
NORFOLK
JONNY X
MAGICK DAGGERS
POINT
JUNCTURE
IWA TORO
VA
NORFOLK
THE DANDY WARHOLS
QUASI

★ transplant from other city

Self-authored work

A great example of a pioneering self-authored project is the magazine *Plazm*. The magazine began in 1991, as a collective effort between writers, designers, and artists. The intention of the founders was to create a publication where "artists represented artists" and included voices and cutting-edge topics not typically heard in the mainstream. The award-winning design studio Plazm, located in Portland, Oregon, designs and publishes the annual magazine which continues to be a premier showcase for art, culture, literary work, and design.

Alternative publications such as zines have created another voice in the art, design, and writing community. Typically, zines are small-run publications (under 5,000 copies), combining text (often handwritten) with images (often hand-drawn or appropriated).

Today's zines continue to allow for multiple types of writing and artwork (computer generated, hand-drawn, illustrated) and typically can cover a wide variety of topics including politics, pop culture, music, art, and design. While many are still assembled with love at the local copy shop, print-on-demand services such as Lulu and blurb have brought a level of sophistication never seen before in independent publishing. Online ezines offer the alternative content of a traditional print zine, with the addition of links, message boards, color photos, video, and animation. Some publications begin their life in one medium and end up in another. One example is the storytelling magazine *Fray*, which began as a website in 1996. Key to its success was how it saw the potentiality of the web as a means of sharing stories. As editor Derek Powazek says, "Every story has a posting area at the end where everyone is invited to tell their own story…. This is one of the things that makes publications on the Web different from any other medium… and, in my opinion, better."[2] Today, *Fray* has changed direction and is now a themed, quarterly print publication, comprised of personal stories and original artwork submitted by readers.

"New hybrid media company" 8020, publisher of the magazines *JPG* and *Everywhere*, develops its content through an active online audience. Each magazine solicits stories and photography from its readers, yet these highly polished magazines are indistinguishable from a Condé Nast production.

DESIGN IT YOURSELF

Finding a way to self-author and publish a book is getting easier with the aforementioned on-demand publishing sites. These services offer an easy and economical way to get your words and images into print and distributed. They can even get you an ISBN (International Standard Book Number), and distribution on Amazon.

The books *D.I.Y. Design it Yourself* and *Indie Publishing: How to Design and Publish* authored by designer, educator, and writer Ellen Lupton and her graduate students at Maryland Institute College of Art and Design, explore the many ways that you can design and publish your own work. Lupton, a champion of the DIY movement, explains that Indie Publishing "is directed at designers, writers, poets, artists... it looks at the process of publishing and also the design aspects of publishing; how to design a novel, how to go about designing a book of poetry."[3]

The DIY movement (video) has truly empowered artists and designers to create and share work like never before.

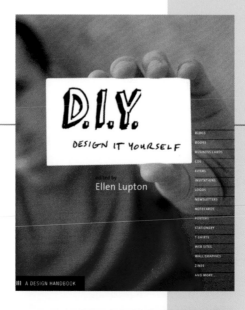

Writing as a voice for design

Twenty or so years ago, graphic design was slowly beginning its transition into computer technology. Prior to 1985, most designers were traditionally trained with the tools of the trade; rulers, t-squares, rubylith, Rapidograph pens, etc. Typesetting was the sole domain of career type-setters, who could quickly set beautiful galleys of type, with equally beautiful rags. The discourse of graphic design was limited.

Clearly, the Internet has changed the way we express our thoughts and opinions and the opportunity for writing and publishing is greater than ever. This democratization of voice, including websites, blogs, videos, and podcasts, has afforded numerous outlets to self-publish. The discipline of graphic design has grown to encompass numerous outlets for self-publishing in a very short time span.

PRINT
1940 – PRESENT

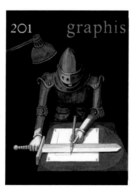

GRAPHIS
1944 – PRESENT

I.D.
1954 – PRESENT

COMMUNICATION ARTS
1959 – PRESENT

Publications such as *Upper & Lower Case, Graphis, Print,* and *Communication Arts* were immensely valuable, as they provided provocative and insightful articles on design history and showcased much of what was happening nationally and internationally within design. The journals *Visible Language,* and *DesignIssues,* launched in the late 1970s, were trailblazers that offered insightful and rigorous writing on design research and theory; and several magazines such as *Design Quarterly, I.D.,* and *Metropolis,* enabled graphic designers to learn about and make connections to other design fields, such as architecture and industrial design. A certain number of annuals, resulting from competitions, such as AIGA *Year in Design, Art Directors Club,* and *Type Directors Club* provided a visual window into the most innovative design of the time, but much of the writing about graphic design was done by a small number of established writers and critics. Design making and design writing seemed to inhabit fairly separate domains. Yet what was missing during this time period, (though most of us did not know it) was a platform for designers throughout the world to speak. Enter *Emigre* magazine.

VISIBLE LANGUAGE
1967 – PRESENT

UPPER & LOWER CASE
1973 – PRESENT

METROPOLIS
1981 – PRESENT

DESIGN ISSUES
1984 – PRESENT

DESIGN QUARTERLY
1946 – 1993

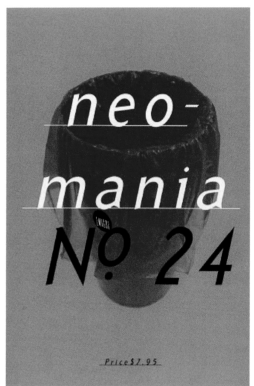

EMIGRE MAGAZINE
1984 - 2005

Emigre swayed from the usual format of showing slick, polished work. Instead, it offered the reader an oversized, two-color magazine that contained both excellent (opinionated) writing and innovative experimentation with layout and typography. Founded in 1984 by Rudy VanderLans and Zuzana Licko, this was a journal that influenced how we look at design writing and discourse today. Another influence is the World Wide Web.

The Internet is unprecedented in opening up a flood of information and publishing possibilities. Websites, wikis, and blogs have continued to develop and include valuable places for individuals to browse, read, write, and voice their thoughts. Blogs are growing at an unprecedented rate, creating a place for worldwide conversations to take place. Blogs have helped bring conversations outside the classroom, and are being used as a way to discuss ideas and visual work.

In recent years, few blogs have been more influential in advancing electronic design discourse than *Design Observer* and *SpeakUp*. Design Observer is a blog devoted to "critical writings on design and culture." Its editors and contributing writers are some of the most respected designers and writers in the field, including Michael Bierut, Rick Poynor, and Lorraine Wild, thus creating a very high level of authorship. *Design Observer* was conceived with the idea of creating a forum that would move beyond graphic designers speaking solely to each other and instead tackle topics that relate to design and culture at large. *SpeakUp* was also instrumental in furthering the conversation of design from within the profession. *SpeakUp's* mission, as stated by founder Armin Vit was to create an "author-based, reader-supported community devoted to graphic design, and open to conversation and dialogue."[4] Its high level of writing, constant energy, and exchange of opinions generated more diversity in voices and opinions. Together with *DesignObserver*, it came to the forefront of creative discourse.

Writer and educator Ellen Lupton points out one advantage of blogs is that they "engage a reader in a different way than print... when you read a blog, you read it with a level of almost prurient interest that you don't have with print, because you know you have the possibility to answer back."[5]

COMMUNITY OF MAKERS

Jessica Helfand and William Drenttel, two of the co-founders of *Design Observer*, launched an award for writing and design criticism in 2006 called the Winterhouse Awards for Design Writing and Criticism. This unique award specifically recognizes young voices in the design community (under 40) with the goal of expanding and elevating writing and design criticism in the 21st century.

Helfand explains "If we cultivate and acknowledge the need for and the benefit of a community of makers who are also writers, we would have a whole new body of writing, one that would begin this new century with a much more robust embrace of the visual world through language."[6] The makers Helfand refers to come from diverse disciplines such as graphic design, fashion, film, and architecture.

An increasing number of innovative masters and even PhD programs in graphic design and design criticism are also popping up. In Fall 2008, The School of Visual Arts launched a new and innovative graduate program in Writing and Design Criticism. The program, the first of its kind in the nation, enables students to explore design from a critical and analytical perspective, giving them the tools to work as design managers, curators, journalists, design critics, and educators.

Chair Alice Twemlow states, comments "The School of Visual Arts MFA in Design Criticism seeks to cultivate design criticism as a discipline and contribute to public discourse with new writing and thinking that is imaginative, historically informed and socially accountable."[7] The two year program culminates with students organizing a public conference, where their work will be presented alongside established design critics and thinkers.

As we continue to broaden our definitions of literacy and explore new ways to approach verbal and visual communication, it is apparent that writing is pivotal. New technologies afford us countless opportunities to bring together both the making and the voicing of ideas. Artists and designers are instrumental in helping shape visual and verbal literacy for the 21st century.

Keep a journal

Paper journals provide a way to write down your thoughts, ideas, and experiences. Online journals work similarly, only all of your writing is done on a computer and kept online. Whichever medium you choose, this type of private writing can help you with your process. Check out these free and private sites:

» 750 words
» ohLife
» Memiary

Zoom in

Take an 8.5" x 11" piece of paper and cut two L's out of it, to form "croppers." Find an image and "zoom in" or crop, to create a new meaning of the original image. Write about the contrast of the old and new meaning formed. There is a set of L croppers on the CD in the back of this book.

Make a blog

Blogs are a great way to get your thoughts and ideas into the public sphere. They are free to set up and easily allow you to share and get quick feedback on a project. There are many sites that make setting up a blog simple, such as Tumblr, Blogspot, or WordPress.

Create a communal poem

Ask five people to give you five words each (just random words that come to their minds quickly). Create one poem from the 25 words you have collected.

Organize your inspiration

Think about ways you might organize that which inspires you. Try creating a sketchbook devoted to textures and color swatches, a flat file that contains cut up images for collages, or an RSS feed that brings together your favorite design blogs. Organizing your inspiration can help you utilize these resources more effectively. Two inspiring sites to gather inspiration are FFFFound.com and Pinterest.com.

WRITING IN PRACTICE

6

As an artist and designer, you will be using writing to present yourself to others, to get projects, and to publicize your work. Artist's statements, résumés, press releases, project briefs, and job applications are some of the ways you will be writing. Though the type of writing may vary, the writing process for the most part remains the same. Like any creative project, a back and forth development and review/feedback process is essential. Begin with figuring out the best process to use for that particular project. Steps may include initial brainstorming, reading, research, observation and analysis, initial draft development, review and editing, continued draft development, final draft, design and layout. The more you see writing as a fluid part of your process, the more confident you will become in expressing yourself in words.

Presenting yourself

Writing helps you publicize yourself and your work. In both art and design, it is necessary to create well-written and designed self-promotional materials, to get your name out, for gallery representation or studio work. Though the goals of an artist and a designer may differ, the professionalism expected of the packet presentation is the same. Creating your own websites and blogs, and contributing to others, can help people see what your work is all about, while at the same time building up your confidence as a writer/artist/designer. In addition to a website, a graphic designer may choose to create a simple promotional piece, such as a postcard, small booklet, or DVD to leave behind with a potential employer. With thousands of talented designers vying for jobs, a well-written and cleverly designed "leave behind" is crucial. Other forms of writing, such as short essays, interviews, and reviews, are valuable in getting your viewpoints out into the community and at the same time helping you strengthen your critical thinking and writing skills.

Artist's packet

For artists, the first step is putting together an artist's packet. The packet is sent to potential galleries and museums when inquiring about representation. It is the first impression a gallery will have of you and your work, and should be professional. Remember that galleries receive dozens of packets each week, so make sure you have taken the time to organize and proof each piece in the packet carefully. Always target those galleries and museums that might best represent your work. The packet, which can be put together and mailed in a large envelope, should contain the following:

» Cover letter
» Artist's Statement
» Résumé
» Bio
» Annotated work samples (name, title of work, media, size and price) as slides and/or digital images on a CD/DVD or website
» Separate sheet with the same annotated information (optional) and reviews of past shows, articles published about your work, exhibition announcements and catalogues
» Self-addressed, stamped envelope

Press packet

A press packet is the same as an artist's packet with the inclusion of a press release, and is used by artists to publicize a gallery show. The press packet can be sent to contacts either electronically (PDF) or through standard mail. It contains several crucial pieces of communication:

» Cover letter
» Artist's Statement
» Résumé
» Bio
» Annotated work samples on a CD/DVD or website Press release
» (optional) Review of shows

Portfolios

For designers, a portfolio is the equivalent of an artist's packet. It is the first impression someone will have of your work. The best portfolios are well-organized, well-structured and well-written. A portfolio can be thought of as a story, with a beginning, middle, and end. Though the portfolio is primarily a vehicle to show off your visual work, close attention should be paid to all aspects, including the writing. Most likely someone will be viewing your work, at least initially, without you sitting there. Make sure your project descriptions are clearly written and proofread. Go further than just describing what the project was (e.g., package or branding). Give the viewer some insight into your concept, your way of thinking and working. Writing a concise project description can be as challenging as writing a one-page design philosophy, so give yourself plenty of time to write multiple drafts.

Digital portfolios

Nick Bauer

Sara Cespedes

Polite Design

Design statement or philosophy

To land a job today, a designer needs much more than a slick portfolio. Employers are interested in hiring designers who have experience working collaboratively, as well as skills in strategic thinking. Writing up a succinct paragraph that addresses these points can help you prepare for the important interview to come. You may also include a version of this statement on your website or within a portfolio. This statement, no more than a paragraph, aims to give the reader some insight into how you think and work. Some points you might cover in this statement: What experience have you had working collaboratively on a team and how has that influenced you? Where do you look for creative inspiration? If you are a recent graduate, refer back to your class projects and think about why you made certain design choices.

Cover letters

Think of a cover letter as an introductory page to a well-written and well-designed package. It should accompany any professional correspondence, from artist's packets and job applications to grant proposals and graduate school applications. The letter can expand on points in your résumé and should end with what specifically you are including in the contents of the package, e.g., résumé, DVD, application, bio. Whether printed or electronic, a letter must concisely describe what is being sent and show attention to detail (spelling, punctuation, addresses). E-mail is not an excuse to be casual. Steven Heller gives some great advice in his article *A Word to the Unwise*. Pay particular attention to the spelling of names. A letter with one or two spelling errors may send your work to the bottom of the pile.

What to do before you write it

Take the time to visit and carefully review the website of the gallery, firm, or studio you are writing to, so that you can explain in your cover letter why you feel the fit is good for you. For an artist, does the gallery represent the type of artist you are? Does it show the medium you work in? Do other artists have a favorable opinion of the gallery? For a designer, ask yourself if the size of the studio is a good fit, does the work of the studio resonate with the type of work you do or would like to do? Include the following in your letter:

» Your return address

» Date line

» Recipient address

» Salutation

» Message

» Complimentary close

» Signature

Good	Bad
keep design simple and elegant	use of too many fonts and design elements
pay attention to all details	paper is wrinkled or smudged
get proofread by at least 2 people	typos (especially names)
re-write and tailor the letter for each inquiry	to have one generic letter do the job for all
keep the letter succinct, one page in length	long-winded and wordy
follow format of other communication pieces	treat each as separate design piece
be specific about what you are asking for (internship, job, etc.)	passive voice or vague phrases
show initiative (e.g., tell them you will call on Monday the 30th)	expect them to call you ("I can be reached at 390-288-8265")
address a specific and correct name in salutation	"To Whom it May Concern"
keep it professional, but friendly	write too informally

Artist statement

An artist's statement is a written narrative that gives some insight into your work. A well-written statement clarifies your ideas and goals and gives the reader a richer view of who you are as an artist. Writing an artist's statement is one of the most challenging but important pieces of writing an artist will do. Be prepared to review and revise multiple times. Once you have a solid piece of writing about your work, you may revise it slightly, if needed, for particular shows.

How it is used

» As an introduction to who you are as an artist and person

» As an introduction to a specific body of work

» As a more general artist's statement

» As part of your packet for a prospective gallery

» As part of a packet for graduate school

» As part of a gallery or museum show (about a specific body of work)

» As part of a grant application

Good	Bad
include concept, content and intent of your work	simply describe the work
keep it succinct: 1–2 pages	use obtuse art terms or sentimental clichés
write clearly and to the point	use excessive adjectives or big words intended to impress
write in first person	begin every sentence with "I"

How to begin

» Create word lists that describe your work and concepts.

» Use freewriting as a way to generate ideas. Ask yourself relevant questions before these such as:

» What were you exploring in this body of work?

» What are some of your goals?

» Why have you chosen this medium to work with?

» What is unique or distinct about your work and creative process?

» What artists have influenced you?

» How might you describe your work and working process?

Résumés (also known as cv's or curricula vitae)

Résumés give a one-page overview of your skills and experience. Keeping the résumé succinct but filled with the most relevant information is crucial. A résumé for a designer should include education, work experience, clients, skills, publications, and awards. A fine artist's should list education, detailed exhibition record (solo and group), grants, awards and commissions, and a bibliography which details which publication reviewed the work and when.

What to do before you write it

Spend some time collecting and writing notes of your experiences, skills, and attributes. Search for people with the job title you want on LinkedIn.com for examples of relevant experience.

Tips

Edit the information to fit on one page.

Collect résumés from others to view format and content.

Think of this as a marketing tool for you: sell yourself through the content and layout. A designer's résumé should demonstrate his/her abilities in typography and layout. An artist's résumé should be simple and clear to make the information accessible.

Tailor résumés to highlight different strengths for each position you are applying to. Make sure you understand the position being listed or opportunity being offered.

Give up-to-date contact information (give two addresses if you are a student or have temporary housing: your current and a permanent one). Résumés often go on file and you want to be found no matter when they might want you.

List your items in a reverse chronological order (most recent first).

Watch your tenses when you are writing: i.e., if you had a job or experience in the past, then write "worked"; if you hold that job now, then write "work." Use action verbs: "created," "produced," "edited."

Use spell check and have two friends proofread. Remember: words can be used wrongly even when they are spelled right!

Good	Bad
keep résumé simple; one or two colors	overuse of decorative elements
logical and clear hierarchy of type	overuse of typefaces, weights, etc.
keep all information relevant and true	pad résumé or give false information
make yourself shine on this one page	list unfavorable information such as 2.0 GPA
write in specifics e.g., "self-motivated"	speak in broad generalizations, e.g., "excellent inter-personal skills"
write "references available upon request"	list two or three reference names

Before

nickname

too many decorative elements

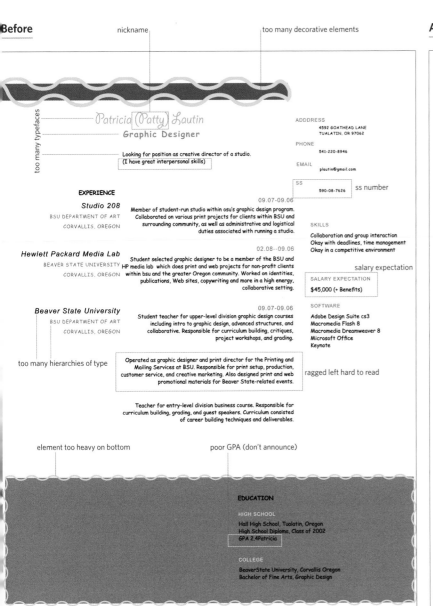

too many typefaces

Patricia (Patty) Lautin
Graphic Designer

Looking for position as creative director of a studio.
(I have great interpersonal skills)

ADDDRESS
4592 GOATHEAD LANE
TUALATIN, OR 97062

PHONE
541-220-8946

EMAIL
plautin@gmail.com

SS
590-08-7626   ss number

EXPERIENCE

09.07-09.06

Studio 208
BSU DEPARTMENT OF ART
CORVALLIS, OREGON

Member of student-run studio within osu's graphic design program. Collaborated on various print projects for clients within BSU and surrounding community, as well as administrative and logistical duties associated with running a studio.

02.08--09.06

Hewlett Packard Media Lab
BEAVER STATE UNIVERSITY
CORVALLIS, OREGON

Student selected graphic designer to be a member of the BSU and HP media lab which does print and web projects for non-profit clients within bsu and the greater Oregon community. Worked on identities, publications, Web sites, copywriting and more in a high energy, collaborative setting.

09.07-09.06

Beaver State University
BSU DEPARTMENT OF ART
CORVALLIS, OREGON

Student teacher for upper-level division graphic design courses including intro to graphic design, advanced structures, and collaborative. Responsible for curriculum building, critiques, project workshops, and grading.

too many hierarchies of type

Operated as graphic designer and print director for the Printing and Mailing Services at BSU. Responsible for print setup, production, customer service, and creative marketing. Also designed print and web promotional materials for Beaver State-related events.

ragged left hard to read

Teacher for entry-level division business course. Responsible for curriculum building, grading, and guest speakers. Curriculum consisted of career building techniques and deliverables.

SKILLS
Collaboration and group interaction
Okay with deadlines, time management
Okay in a competitive environment

salary expectation

SALARY EXPECTATION
$45,000 (+ Benefits)

SOFTWARE
Adobe Design Suite cs3
Macromedia Flash 8
Macromedia Dreamweaver 8
Microsoft Office
Keynote

element too heavy on bottom

poor GPA (don't announce)

EDUCATION

HIGH SCHOOL
Hall High School, Tualatin, Oregon
High School Diploma, Class of 2002
GPA 2.4Patricia

COLLEGE
BeaverState University, Corvallis Oregon
Bachelor of Fine Arts, Graphic Design

After

Patricia Lautin
Graphic Designer

ADDRESS
4592 GOATHEAD LANE
TUALATIN,OR 97062

PHONE
542-220-8946

EMAIL
PLAUTIN@GMAIL.COM

EXPERIENCE

Studio 208   09.07-PRESENT
BSU DEPARTMENT OF ART
CORVALLIS, OREGON

Member of student-run studio within BSU's graphic design program. Collaborated on various print projects for clients within BSU and surrounding community, as well as administrative and logistical duties associated with running a studio.

Hewlett Packard Media Lab   02.08-PRESENT
BEAVER STATE UNIVERSITY
CORVALLIS, OREGON

Student selected graphic designer to be a member of the BSU and HP media lab which does print and web projects for non-profit clients within BSU and the greater Oregon community. Worked on identities, publications, Web sites, copywriting and more in a high energy, collaborative setting.

Beaver State University   09.07-PRESENT
BSU DEPARTMENT OF ART
CORVALLIS, OREGON

Student teacher for upper-level division graphic design courses including intro to graphic design, advanced structures, and collaborative. Responsible for curriculum building, critiques, project workshops, and grading.

Printing and Mailing Co.   09.06-03.07
BEAVER STATE UNIVERSITY
CORVALLIS, OREGON

Operated as graphic designer and print director for the Printing and Mailing Services at BSU. Responsible for print setup, production, customer service, and creative marketing. Also designed print and web promotional materials for Beaver State-related events.

Oregon State University   09.05-12.05
BSU DEPARTMENT OF BUSINESS
CORVALLIS, OREGON

Teacher for entry-level division business course. Responsible for curriculum building, grading, and guest speakers. Curriculum consisted of career building techniques and deliverables.

EDUCATION

HIGH SCHOOL
Hall High School, Tualatin, Oregon
High School Diploma, Class of 2002
Accumulative GPA 3.52
　　　Honors Program

COLLEGE
Beaver State University, Corvallis Oregon
Bachelor of Fine Arts, Graphic Design
BFA Minor, Art History
Graphic Design GPA 3.82
　　　Teacher's Assistant: Art 225 Introduction to Graphic Design
　　　Teacher's Assistant: Art 327 Advanced Typography Structures
　　　Teacher's Assistant: Art 325 Collaborative
　　　Collegiate member of the American Institute of Graphic Arts

SKILLS
Collaboration and group interaction
Comfortable with deadlines, time management
Comfortable in a competitive environment
Cross-platform computer ability
Presentation skills and writing proficiency
Typography and type design
Branding and identity systems
Magazine Layout
Grid Systems
Web Design and interactivity
Semiotics and narrative
Information design
Divergence in process
Ideation and prototyping
Bookbinding

SOFTWARE
Adobe Design Suite cs3
Macromedia Flash 8
Macromedia Dreamweaver 8
Microsoft Office
Keynote

LECTURES & WORKSHOPS ATTENDED
Scott Nash CRANBROOK
Rick Vallecenti TWIST
Elliot Peter Earls CRANBROOK
Gail Swanlund
Colin Metcalf / Kevin Grady C153M

AWARDS
Graphic Design Excellence Award PSN
AIGA Icograda First Place Design TUW
Graphic Design Excellence Award 2002
Honors College 2002, 2009

Press release

A press release may be used to publicize your show to the periodical media (such as newspapers, radio, television, blogs, magazines). It should be concise (no more than one or two pages) and explain the key elements of your show:

» Who is having the show
» Where it is (include URL)
» When it is
» Paragraph or two about the show and the artist
» Contact for further information

Blog entries

In the blogosphere, the opportunity to add your voice to the conversation abounds. A blog post about a particular theme or your work is a great way to get your thoughts down in writing and get them published in a short amount of time. You can also participate in group blogs and online magazines to create awareness for your blog. With that said, a few tips can make your writing stronger.

Tips

Use standard punctuation and capitalization.

Considering the instability of web services, it's always a good idea to type a draft of your comment in a separate document, proof it, and then copy/paste it into the blog. Your entry will be more credible if there are no typos.

Be considerate and respectful.

Stay on theme.

Spell names correctly.

Reference when needed. Though much of blogging contains personal opinions, a well-written point or argument can hold up even better if a reference or two is attached.

Good	Bad
keep on theme with your commentary	write a long rant without substance
proofread	have typos
be respectful	insult and act superior

Grant proposals

Say you have an exciting project you want to undertake—something that is important for you as an artist or designer and perhaps others in the community. The problem is, you don't have enough money to make it happen. Here's where your ability to write a clear and professional grant proposal comes into play. There are many agencies at the local, national, and international level that are interested in funding exciting and important art and design projects. Audience research is part of good writing, so make sure your project is a good fit with the agencies you are applying to, and then present a convincing argument in document form (which should be both well-written and well-presented). Often the first step is writing a solid project narrative.

Project narrative

The project narrative is the meat-and-potatoes of the grant. It clearly and succinctly describes the project, its goals, and why this project should be funded. It is important to realize that the panel reading your proposal may not have expertise in your discipline, and you should show them that you do. Also consider that they read hundreds of proposals, and you need to make yours stand above the rest. Remember, the first couple of paragraphs are most important—if your initial paragraphs are vague or wordy, a panel member will not read the proposal further. An old writer's trick is to look at the first paragraph and see if it can be removed. Many times, the first paragraph you write is your warm up, and can be removed once it has served its purpose. As in journalism, your lead (the first few sentences) is your one chance to grab the committee members' attention. Since they often read hundreds of proposals, assume that they will only decide to continue reading based on those opening paragraphs.

Write a compelling narrative that addresses all of the points asked, including:

» Project objectives: why is this project important and why should it be funded?

» Approach: what approach will you be taking for this project? What medium will you be using and why?

» Project timeline (be realistic)

» Budget (be realistic, don't inflate it)

» Credentials (your credentials are very important on a grant and they will be checked)

» References: a reference letter from a well-known and respected educator, artist, or designer lends clout to your project. Think carefully about who can best speak about you and your project.

Tips

Keep your process organized—there will most likely be many pieces to the grant application including the proposal narrative, work samples, budget, résumé, and letters of reference.

Read through the criteria carefully and give yourself enough time to prepare all materials requested.

Create several drafts of the project narrative and have someone read each draft for understanding and clarity. You should also read it out loud.

Make sure you address all the questions. Re-typing the headings of the outline the agency supplies in the proposal request in that order can ensure you have covered all the necessary points.

Find a contact (sometimes called a project officer) at the funding agency. Often, grant agencies are more than willing to talk to you and answer questions about your project. These agencies are a resource since they want the best grant proposals to be submitted.

Proofread carefully. The review committee could interpret one or two misspelled words as lack of attention to detail.

Make sure you follow all the presentation guidelines. You might wish they could be flexible on type size and margins, but if the guidelines requested it, the review committee could interpret any deviation as lack of willingness to take direction. You don't want to create that perception when you are asking them to entrust you with money to be spent only according to the agreement being created.

Create a unified presentation of all materials (e.g., same typeface, same paper used throughout). Be prepared to follow up if you are not funded. Many times an agency will give feedback on your grant proposal and that is valuable if you choose to resubmit.

Getting business

Designers are in business, and getting business entails a lot of writing. As stated earlier, portfolios and leave-behind promotional materials are essential in getting your work noticed, but once you land the job, the writing really begins. There are several important pieces of writing designers use when working with clients, including project proposals and design briefs. These are usually multiple-page documents intended to explain a project. With a proposal, a designer is attempting to land the job, while a design brief establishes the details of a project already secured. As with most writing, the best proposals are well organized and touch upon each relevant point, using only as many words as necessary. Long-winded proposals and briefs not only waste everyone's time, but will confuse the client as to what you are going to provide.

Proposals

Proposals are common to most design projects and range in length from a simple, one page, bulleted list to a more lengthy narrative, or a combination of both. In essence, the document is proposing the details of the project. In order to write a well-organized pro-posal, and to fully understand the scope of the project, a proposal is often written up after an initial client meeting. Clarify any questions you might have with the client, in order to make the proposal as complete as possible. It is a good idea to have an opening sum-mary statement in your proposal, so that you and the client are on the same page.

Common sections of a proposal include:

» Opening summary

(summarizing what the scope of the project is)

» Problem statement

» Your approach

» To-do list

(showing the client all aspects of what you will do)

» Breakdown of specific phases. For example:

Phase 1: initial presentation of concept sketches

Phase 2: presentation of refined concept

Phase 3: revisions

Phase 4: production and delivery

» Timeline

» Budget

Remember, you are often competing with others to land a job, so don't be lazy! As well as following the rules for résumés and grant proposals, consider taking the time to write up a compelling problem statement. This is a one- to three-paragraph explanation of the challenges the client is facing. It's a chance to show the client you are listening to them, and understand what they are about to undertake. Your approach can show the other side of the coin: how you will then solve those problems you have so masterfully described. Proposals have been won and lost over these sections. Budget is probably the section designers agonize over the most. It's useful to get a book like the *Graphic Artist's Guild Handbook: Pricing & Ethical Guidelines* to advise you on the mysteries of estimating and fix bid vs. time and materials.

Finally, try to avoid doing example solutions. The proposal comes before you fully understand the client, and can often mislead the client. With words, the client can imagine designs that the two of you will eventual-ly create. With pictures they may just think you don't get it. Strangely enough, words—not pictures—may be your greatest ally in getting design work.

Requests for proposal (RFP)

A request for proposal, more commonly known as an RFP, is one way design jobs are awarded. Unlike a standard project proposal, an RFP is a written document prepared by the client, used to solicit proposals by designers for that project. The RFP may be announced to a large group (sometimes referred to as a cattle call) or to a select few studios—it depends on what sort of response the client wishes to elicit. This competitive process allows a client to see many different directions before choosing one studio to work with. An RFP may also be generated from within a firm or studio, to solicit proposals for specific parts of a large project (i.e. a commercial to accompany a brand launch).

As an in-house designer or design manager, you may well take a hand in writing an RFP when you wish to bring in outside help on major projects. This is often your opportunity to set the tone of the working relationship with a studio, and as such it's a good place to lay out your expectations. Common sections of an RFP include:

» Statement of purpose

» Background information

» Scope of work

» Deliverables

» Schedule

» Budget

Design brief (*creative or project brief*)

The purpose of a written design brief is to define the strategy, specific details and goals of a project between the designer and the client. The most effective briefs are really a collaboration between designer and client and may take several back and fourth rounds to get it right. The great thing about a well written, creative brief is that it ensures that the entire project team is on the same page with objectives and expectations.

There is really no standard format for a creative brief, due to the variety of design disciplines and the scope of the project, but a well-written three-page brief is better than a vague and wordy 10-page brief. A brief can be formatted as bulleted information or in a more narrative form, or a combination of both.

The following sections are key to a design brief:

» Project overview, sometimes called an executive summary (a paragraph or two that succinctly explains the purpose of the project)

» Description of target audience

» Communication/business objectives, strategies and goals of the project

» Overview of client's competitors

» Budget and schedule

» Explanation of internal approval process

» Clarification of procedural requirements or limitations

Case studies

There are many ways designers present their finished work to a wider audience, but often a digital portfolio on a website allows for the most exposure. By letting a new audience in on the pertinent details of what you have done for a client, you are helping them understand what you are capable of. Some of the basic components to include when presenting your project as a case study are:

» Quality photographs of your project, showing different aspects (such as overview and details).

» Basic information about the client's situation and communication needs

» Details of services provided (who did what)

Smashing Magazine
AIGA Case Studies

More ways to write

As you read through the latest art and design journals, you will see a wide variety of writing, including expository and opinion essays, researched articles, interviews, and reviews. Often these essays are focused on a particular topic. When you recognize the structure of an essay and what makes it interesting, you can use your understanding to improve your own writing.

Expository essays explain or "expose" a subject or topic. An expository essay examines something in detail, with a more neutral tone than a persuasive or argumentative essay would. The best expository essays don't simply reiterate what has been said about a subject. Rather, they present a well-written analysis of the subject that helps the reader see the subject in a new context.

"Thank You for Not Smoking"
Ralph Caplan, *Voice: AIGA Journal of Design*

Opinion essays may also be labeled argumentative essays or persuasive essays. Writing your opinions is a way to share your voice with a community. Opinion essays can be found in op-ed columns in newspapers, articles in magazines and journals (both online and print), and blogs. Opinion essays state a position on a particular topic, followed with evidence to support the argument or point. It can help to broadly know your target audience when writing the essay. These essays use both your own opinion, as well as researched material.

"We Are All Emerging Economies Now"
John Thakara, *Design Observer*

"It's How You Said It"
Paula Scher, *Design Observer*

Research essays can also be persuasive in nature, and there is typically a thesis statement that helps the reader understand the stance the author takes based on their research. The thesis statement is typically found in the first or second paragraph of the essay. Research essays contain footnotes and may also have a bibliography.

"Bathrooms and Kitchens"
Ellen Lupton and J. Abbott Miller
Design Writing Research

Interviews allow readers to gain a more personal sense of how a person works and thinks. A good interview is a conversation between the writer and the person being interviewed. When interviewing someone, begin by making a long list of questions you might want to ask and narrow those down to 8–10 questions that best represent the topic. Remember that a person may answer two or three questions you've prepared in one answer, so be prepared with follow-up questions. It is also a good practice to send the interviewee the questions ahead of time, so they can prepare thoughtful answers. The best interviews use prepared questions as a guide and allow spontaneity to occur.

"Devil in the Details: An Interview with Esther K. Smith"
Steven Heller, *Voice: AIGA Journal of Design*

"Power to the Panels: An Interview with Paul Buhle"
Michael Dooley, *Voice: AIGA Journal of Design*

Reviews are written to give the reader a sense of what a book, film, play, or gallery/museum show is about. What makes a review different from a neutral description is that the author interjects his or her opinion throughout the review. Reviews are often seen in newspapers, in magazines, and on blogs.

The Back of the Napkin
Dan Roam
Reviewed by Robert Blinn, *Core77*

How to Think Like a Great Graphic Designer
Debbie Millman
Reviewed by Robert Blinn, *Core77*

Critics' picks: *Artforum*

There are plenty of websites that accept submissions, such as essays, blog entries, and reviews. The following are good starting places:

Core77

Sitepoint

A Brief Message

Design Observer

Boxes and Arrows

A List Apart

Voice: AIGA Journal of Design

Getting your projects noticed, finding employment, clients, or representation in a gallery, or starting your own studio involves a lot of hard work, creativity, and writing. Find the best way to practice your writing and start to integrate writing into your process and work. The high quality presentation you put forth of yourself and your work will be noticed.

You may have been drawn to your career choice because of a passion for the visual. You may see verbal expression as an unavoidable obligation. But writing is more than a burden—it is a critical component of your work. Embrace it. You can clarify your thoughts with an outline, share your experiences in a blog, get funding with a proposal. Set aside a bit of time each day for reading and writing, even if you just note an impression or a thought on paper. Writing is a muscle, and needs regular exercise to be strong so it's there when you need it. From the experience of writing in the process of learning to the experience of writing as a business tool, writing is essential to nourishing your creative life.

Question yourself

Interviews are a great way to get to know how a person thinks. Find an interview with an artist or designer who inspires you. After reading the interview, turn the interview around and ask yourself those very same questions.

Make lists

List 10 things you would NOT say in an artist's statement.
List 10 things you would NOT say in a cover letter.
List 10 things you would NOT say in your résumé.

Observe a stranger

Observe a stranger for a few minutes and think about five questions you would want to ask them. Try answering the questions based on your observations of the person.

Deconstruct an image

Think of an image or a piece of art or design that you like. Why do you like it? Analyze the piece and write about its inherent contradictions and tensions. Now put the image that inspired you aside, and try to create a visual piece that somehow responds to your writing in some way.

Student examples

Writing in the classroom can occur in many ways. From writing exercises that can help shape a project to the generation of written content for projects, there are wonderful opportunities for students to work with words and images.

The following projects use writing throughout the process and in the final realization. You can view them on the CD included with the book or at your Peachpit account page (peachpit.com).

North Carolina State University

School of Visual Arts

Oregon State University

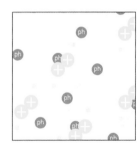

Washington University

University of Houston

University of the Arts

The Ohio State University

Podcasts

These interviews with leading artists, designers, educators, writers, and thinkers focus on the role writing plays in each of their lives. Listen to these podcasts on the CD or download them by going to your Peachpit account page (peachpit.com).

Meredith Davis

Steven Heller

Jessica Helfand

Ellen Lupton

Joshua Berger

Warren Lehrer

The following project was part of a sophomore class assignment at Oregon State University. This three-week poster project, announcing a play for Portland Center Stage, uses various forms of writing to develop ideas and connections throughout the project. This was the third and final project of the term.

The project

Part 1

Students use a word and its opposite as a jumping-off point to write a one-page fiction or non-fiction narrative. (In this case, the word was "play" and the opposite word chosen was "work.") By developing a concept based on their own writing, students not only take more ownership of content, but also see the power of the written word, while building confidence in their writing abilities.

Part 2

The next step to visually translate the narrative. Concepts such as hyperbole, irony, metaphor, narrative, denotation, connotation, allegory, and analogy are discussed in relation to visual communication. By discussing these words, students begin to see the relationships between written communication and visual communication. An important outcome was for students to develop a better understanding of abstracting a visual idea, and much of that understanding came about through writing.

Most importantly, they learn how to abstract an idea visually. Ideas are then written up in a simple, well-designed brief that is presented to peers. Having students solidify their thoughts on paper helps them gain more confidence with writing.

Part 3

The last step of the process involves various idea generation exercises such as mind mapping and freewriting to flush out the essence of the message further. Ongoing discussions and critiques using writing help solidify the poster. The final poster is printed (18"x24") and presented with the process at the critique.

words: play | work
Collage sketch contrasting an image of play with one of work. This was the jumping off point for the written narrative.

Project: Morgan Harrington
Faculty: Christine Gallagher/Andrea Marks

Day after day, all I see is the shiny metal casings of the bombs. It is my job to tighten the screw that seals the cap on the end. Three quick turns and then I place the bomb, standing upright, right next to the last one. I reach for another, insert the screw and turn, turn, turn to until it's tight. I don't think of much else and I don't stop moving. Except yesterday. Yesterday there was a moment when I turned the screw once, twice and there it was: the clear moment of a memory. It's me at ten years old and I'm pedaling as fast as I can down the sloping hill that leads right to my driveway. Maximum speed now! If I'm going fast enough, I can coast all the way up the driveway right to the front door. Then the memory closes. I'm turning the screw as I catch a peek to see if the floor manager has noticed I had stopped working.

This three-week project was from a sophomore class called Graphic Design Processes. The course is designed to guide students through a variety of thinking and making experiments and exercises. Writing in tandem with sketching was used in the process of this project as well as in the final realization.

The project

Students worked with a Dollar Tree object for the entire term (in this case, a lightbulb) and had to do a series of investigations into the object, from its history to its form and cultural significance.

The final project, an 18"x24" poster, examined aspects of information design and how designers translate complex information into exciting visual material.

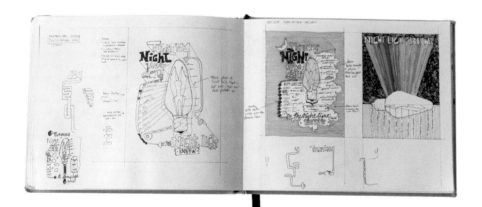

Project: Todd Conger
Faculty: Christine Gallagher/Andrea Marks

Notes

The writer's toolbox

1 A key figure in the field of creative thinking is Edward de Bono. His research in the concept of lateral thinking and his Six Thinking Hats technique have changed the way individuals and businesses approach creative problem-solving. www.en.wikipedia.org/wiki/Six_Thinking_Hats (www.debonogroup.com)

2 Gelb, Michael J. *How to Think Like Leonardo da Vinci.* Delacorte Press, 1998, pp 57–58.

3 One of the people most closely associated with mind mapping is the British psychologist Tony Buzan. Buzan studied the brain and hemispheric symmetry research of neuroscientist Roger Sperry. As a result of this and related research, Buzan developed a technique for utilizing the "whole brain" when generating ideas, which he called the Mind Map®. www.managementconsultingnews.com/interviews/buzan_interview.php

4 Novak, Joseph D. and Gowin, Bob D. *Learning How to Learn.* Cambridge University Press, 1984, pp 15–35.

5 Meredith Davis conversation with the author, May 2008.

6 www.literarytraveler.com/authors/jack_kerouac_scroll.aspx

7 Elbow, Peter. *Everyone Can Write: Essays Toward a Hopeful Theory of Writing and Teaching Writing.* Oxford University Press, 2000, pp 85–92.

8 www.mycoted.com/Brainwriting

9 Gelb, Michael J. *How to Think Like Leonardo DaVinci.* Delacorte Press, 1998, pp 224–228.

10 www.theatlantic.com/doc/199512/edison

11 Michalko, Michael. *Cracking Creativity.* Berkeley: Ten Speed Press, 2001, p 105.

12 Julio Torres Lara, discussion with the author, April 2008.

Thinking in words and pictures

1 Edwards, Betty. *Drawing on the Right Side of the Brain.* Los Angeles: J.P. Tarcher, 1979, pp 26, 27.

2 Edwards pp 27–29.

3 Professor Enriqueta Canseco-Gonzalez, cognitive neuroscientist at Reed College, Portland, Oregon, conversation with the author, November, 2007.

4 www.vark-learn.com

5 Koberg, Don, and Bagnall, Jim, *The Universal Traveler; a Soft-Systems Guide to Creativity, Problem-Solving, & the Process of Reaching Goals.* Los Altos, California: Crisp Learning, 1991, p 26.

6 Number 3 of Bruce Mau's *"Incomplete Manifesto for Growth,"* written in 1998, www.brucemaudesign.com/incomplete_manifesto.html

7 IDEO.com

8 Koberg & Bagnall, p 27.

9 "The Hidden Secrets of the Creative Mind," interview with Dr. R. Keith Sawyer, Time.com, January 8, 2006.

10 De Bono, Edward. *Lateral thinking: creativity step by step.* New York: Harper & Row, 1990, p 64.

Verbal and visual connections

1 Faigley, Lester and others. *Picturing Texts*. New York: Norton, 2004, pp 14–19.

2 Merriam-Webster Online Dictonary

3 Paul, Richard and Elder, Linda. *Critical & Creative Thinking*. California: The Foundation for Critical Thinking, 2004, p 40.

4 Wikipedia, en.wikipedia.org/wiki/Amazon_Kindle

5 Kelly, Kevin, "Scan This Book," *The New York Times*, July 16, 2006.

6 Kelly, p 45.

7 Kelly, p 45.

Narrative structures:
verbal and visual working together

1 Trollbäck, Jakob, "One Designer Shares: How to Use Design to Tell a Story," Howdesign.com www.howdesign.com/article/storytelling/, January 23, 2008.

2 Tufte, Edward, "PowerPoint is Evil," *Wired*, September 2003. www.wired.com/wired/archive/11.09/ppt2.html

3 Azab Powell, Bonnie, "David Byrne Really Does ❤ PowerPoint," *UC Berkeley News*, March 8, 2005. berkeley.edu/news/media/releases/2005/03/08_byrne.shtml

4 Byrne, David, "Learning to Love Powerpoint," *Wired*, September 2003. www.wired.com/wired/archive/11.09/ppt1.html

5 Warren Lehrer, interview with the author, November 7, 2007.

6 www.en.wikipedia.org/wiki/Hypertext_fiction

7 www.en.wikipedia.org/wiki/Graphic_novel

Writing and editing in the 21st century

1 Drenttel, William, "The Written Word: Design as Mediator," *Graphic Design and Reading: Explorations of an Uneasy Relationship*, ed. Gunnar Swanson. New York: Allworth Press, 2000, pp 167–169.

2 www.fray.com/about/

3 Ellen Lupton, interview with the author, December 18, 2007.

4 Vit, Armin, www.underconsideration.com/speakup/

5 Ellen Lupton, interview with the author, December 18, 2007.

6 Jessica Helfand, interview with the author, July 24, 2007.

7 Twemlow, Alice, www.schoolofvisualarts.edu/grad

Resources
Design/Culture

A Brief Message

A List Apart

ArtJob

Art Network

Art Papers

Artsy

Behance

Boxes and Arrows

Coroflot

Concept Share

Design Observer

Design Writing Research

ffffound

ideasonideas

mediabistro

UnBeige

Under Consideration

Veer

Veerle's blog

Voice: AIGA Journal of Design

Writing resources: electronic

A Writer's Reference
Bedford Bibliographer
Scrivener
Write Room

Writing resources: books

A Pocket Style Manual by Diana Hacker
Artful Sentences: Syntax as Style by Virginia Tufte
A Whole New Mind by Daniel H. Pink
Clear and Simple as the Truth by Francis-Noel Thomas
Creating the Perfect Design Brief by Peter L. Phillips
EasyWriter: A Pocket Guide by Andrea Lunsford and
  Robert Connors
Figures of Speech: 60 Ways to Turn a Phrase
  by Arthur Quinn
Graphic Storytelling and Visual Narrative by Will Eisner
How to be an Explorer of the World by Keri Smith
How to Do Things with Words by J.L. Austin
*Kant and the Platypus: Essays on Language
and Cognition* by Umberto Eco
Made to Stick by Chip and Dan Heath
On Writing Well by William Zinsser
Oulipo: A Primer of Potential Literature
  by Warren F. Motte Jr.
Poetical Dictionary by Lohren Green
Research and Documentation in the Electronic Age
  by Diana Hacker
Studies in the Way of Words by Paul Grice
Style: Ten Lessons in Clarity and Grace
  by Joseph Williams
Taking the Leap; Building a Career as a Visual Artist
  by Cay Lang

The Artist's Guide by Jackie Battenfield
The Craft of Research by Wayne Booth, Gregory Colomb,
  and Joseph Williams
The Observation Deck by Naomi Epel
The Craft of Revision by Donald M. Murray
The Elements of Style by William Strunk Jr. and E.B. White
  (illustrated by Maira Kalman)
The Graphic Designer's Guide to Better Business Writing
  by Barbara Janoff and Ruth Cash-Smith
The Politics of Writing by Romy Clark and Roz Ivanic
Understanding Comics by Scott McCloud
Why I Have Not Written Any of My Books
  by Marcel Benabou
Woe is I by Patricia T. O'Conner
Writing About Art by Henry Sayre
Writing Down the Bones by Natalie Goldberg
Writing with Power by Peter Elbow
Writing to Learn by William Zinsser
99 Ways to Tell a Story: Exercises in Style
  by Matt Madden

Publishing resources

D.I.Y. Design It Yourself by Ellen Lupton
Indie Publishing by Ellen Lupton
Lulu
Blurb
One Story
Fray
JPG
MagCloud
Plazm

Bibliography

Bamford, Anne. *The Visual Literacy White Paper.* Commissioned by Adobe Systems Pty Ltd, Australia, Art and Design University of Technology, Sydney.

Baron, Naomi. *Alphabet to Email: How Written Language Evolved and Where it's Heading.* London: Routledge, 2000.

Bernstein, Mashey, George Yatchisin. *Writing for the Visual Arts.* Upper Saddle River, New Jersey: Prentice Hall, 2001.

Crow, Gerald. "The Writing Problems of Visual Thinkers." *Visible Language* 28.2(1994): pp 134–161.

de Bono, Edward. *Lateral thinking: creativity step by step.* New York: Harper & Row, 1990.

Denton, Craig. *Graphics for Visual Communication.* Dubuque, Iowa: Wm. C Brown Publishers, 1992.

Drenttel, William. "The Written Word: the Designer as Mediator." *Graphic Design & Reading: Explorations of an Uneasy Relationship.* Ed. Gunnar Swanson. New York: Allworth Press, 2000.

Edwards, Betty. *Drawing on the Right Side of the Brain.* Los Angeles: J.P. Tarcher, 1979

Elbow, Peter. *Writing with Power: Techniques for Mastering the Writing Process.* New York: Oxford University Press, 1998.

Faigley, Lester, Diana George, Anna Palchik, Cynthia Selfe. *Picturing Texts.* New York: W.W. Norton & Company, 2004.

Gelb, Michael. *How to Think like Leonardo da Vinci.* New York: Delacorte, 1998.

Janoff, Barbara, and Ruth Cash-Smith. *The Graphic Designer's Guide to Better Business Writing.* New York: Allworth Press, 2007.

Koberg, Don, and Jim Bagnall. *The Universal Traveler: A Soft-Systems Guide to Creativity, Problem-Solving, and the Process of Reaching Goals.* Menlo Park, California: Crisp Learning.

Odell, Lee, and Susan M. Katz. *Writing in a Visual Age.* New York: Bedford /St. Martin's, 2006.

Lang, Cay. *Taking the Leap; Building a Career as a Visual Artist.* San Francisco: Chronicle Books, 2006.

Laurel, Brenda, ed. *Design Research: Methods and Perspectives.* Cambridge, MA: The MIT Press, 2003.

Lawson, Bryan. *How Designers Think.* 2nd ed. London: Butterworth Architecture, 1990.

Lusser Rico, Gabriele. *Writing the Natural Way: Using Right-Brain Techniques to Release Your Expressive Powers.* Los Angeles: J.P. Tarcher, Inc., 1983.

McCloud, Scott. *Understanding Comics: The Invisible Art.* New York: HarperPerennial, 1994.

Nystrand, Martin. *What Writers Know: the Language, Process, and Structure of Written Discourse.* New York: Academic Press, 1982.

Paul, Dr. Richard, and Dr. Linda Elder. *The Nature and Functions of Critical and Creative Thinking.* The Thinker's Guide Library. Dillon Beach, California: The Foundation for Critical Thinking, 2004.

Phillips, Peter L. *Creating the Perfect Design Brief: How to Manage Design for Strategic Advantage.* New York: Allworth Press, 2004.

Ruggiero, Vincent. *The Art of Critical Thinking: A Guide to Critical and Creative Thought.* 7th ed. New York: Longman, 2004.

Ruszkiewicz, Daniel, Daniel Anderson, and Christy Friend. *Beyond Words, Reading and Writing in a Visual Age.* New York: Pearson/Longman, 2006.

Sharples, Mike. *How We Write; Writing as Creative Design.* London: Routledge, 1999.

Strunk, William, Jr., and E.B. White. *The Elements of Style.* New York: The Penguin Press, 2005.

Walston, Mark. "When Words and Images Collide." *Voice:* AIGA *Journal of Design.* April 12, 2006. www.voice.aiga.org

West, Thomas G. *In the Mind's Eye: Visual Thinkers, Gifted People With Dyslexia and Other Learning Difficulties, Computer Images and Ironies of Creativity.* Amherst, New York: Prometheus Books, 1997.

Zaidel, Dahlia. *Neuropsychology of Art: Neurological, Congitive and Evolutionary Perspectives.* New York: Psychology Press, 2005.

Zinsser, William. *Writing to Learn.* New York: Harper and Row, 1989.

Image credits

Cover image: ©Julio Torres Lara

Page 2 Photo: Andrea Marks

Page 4 Mind map: Todd Conger

Page 6 Concept map: Morgan Harrington/ Grace Noel

Page 8 Kerouac Scroll: courtesy of Christie's of New York

Page 12/13 Photos: Joe Carolina

Page 14 Photo: Andrea Marks

Page 15 Pages from the field diaries kept by Prof. R. Good. The data was used towards the publication of his "Geographical Handbook of the Dorset Flora" (1948). Courtesy: Dorset Environmental Records Centre

Page 18 Photo: ©Lee Cullivan

Page 19 Photo: Joe Carolina

Page 22 Photo: Andrea Marks

Page 25 Sketchbooks: Julio Torres Lara

Page 27 Edison telephone: ©Hulton Archive/ Getty Images

Page 29 Edison Idelia ©2008 by Auction Team Breker, Cologne, Germany

Page 31 Experimental sound made for Edison's Kinetophone, Library of Congress

Page 40 image: Brain illustration: http://etc.usf.edu/clipart/

Page 41 Brain illustration: Google Images

Page 44 Photo: Joe Carolina

Page 49 Photo: ©IDEO

Page 51 Photo: ©Alistair Bird

Page 60 Photo: ©Tom Matthew

Page 63 Photo: ©Samantha Armacost

Page 65 Photo: Joe Carolina

Page 74 ©Warren Lehrer
Crossing the BLVD: Strangers, Neighbors, Aliens in a New America, 2003. Conceived and written by Warren Lehrer and Judith Sloan. Design and photography by Warren Lehrer. Published by W.W. Norton. crossingtheblvd.org Book documents and portrays new immigrants and refugees in the most polyglot locality in the United States.

Page 71 ©Warren Lehrer
French Fries, 1984. Written by Dennis Bernstein and Warren Lehrer and designed by Warren Lehrer. Published by Visual Studies Workshop Press and EarSay. A play/book that takes place at a fast-food joint on a winter's day at the height of the Cold War.

Page 75 From *Hellboy: Wake the Devil* ™ ©2011 Mike Mignola. All rights reserved. Used with permission and courtesy of Dark Horse Comics.

Page 85 Poster: PDX Music Memory ©*Plazm* Art director: Joshua Berger Design: Linda Reynen Editors: Jon Raymond, Tiffany Lee Brown *Plazm* Magazine, Issue #29

Page 87 Cover design: *D.I.Y. Design It Yourself*, Mike Weikert, Nancy Froehlich, Kristen Spilman, *D.I.Y. Kids*, Nancy Froehlich

Page 88 Cover image courtesy of *Print* Magazine

Page 88 Cover image courtesy of *Graphis* Magazine

Page 88 Cover Art by Tomi Ungerer, 1979, Issue #201

Page 88 Cover image courtesy of *I.D.* Magazine

Page 88 Cover image: Dominique Malaterre, TILT Reprinted with permission by *Communication Arts* ©2008 Coyne & Blanchard, Inc. All rights reserved.

Page 89 Cover image courtesy of *Visible Language*

Page 89 Cover image courtesy of *U&lc*

Page 89 Cover image courtesy of *Metropolis*

Page 89 Cover image courtesy of *DesignIssues*

Page 89 Cover image courtesy of Walker Art Center

Page 90 Covers courtesy of *Emigre*

Page 93 Photo: Joe Carolina

Acknowledgments

This book has been in the making for a very long time and so my acknowledgments date back to 1995, when I was asked to teach my first Writing Intensive Curriculum (WIC) course at Oregon State University. Due to a university-wide mandate, every undergraduate was required to take a WIC course in his or her major. Suddenly, my comfort zone of teaching graphic design was challenged by the task of how to bring more writing into the classroom.

So, my first thanks go to my university for passing that mandate. Next I want to thank Vicki Tolar Burton, who runs the Writing Intensive Curriculum program at OSU. Vicki's faculty workshops are key to helping empower faculty as they find new ways to add writing to their curriculum. Through an OSU WIC grant, I was able to develop a self-published book titled *Graphic Design and Writing: A Student Guide*, which became the impetus for *Writing for Visual Thinkers*.

I am grateful that Peachpit is a publisher with vision. The entire team at Peachpit, including publisher Nancy Aldrich-Ruenzel, managing editor Lupe Edgar, production editor Hilal Sala, publicist Laura Ross, and marketing manager Sara Jane Todd, have patiently and thoughtfully answered all of my questions and guided me through some new territory.

In particular, I would like to thank Michael Nolan, acquisitions editor at Peachpit Press, for lending an ear to my book proposal pitch on a chance meeting at the 2005 AIGA National Design Conference in Boston. His input and support in developing the project, initially as an ebook and now as a print book, were critical and are much appreciated. I would also like to thank Sue Apfelbaum, editorial director at AIGA, for her insight and guidance throughout this process. Big thanks go to Christina Wodtke, my content development editor on the first edition, for her inspiration, invaluable input, and advice in helping shape the content; and to my copy editor Rose Weisburd, who questioned, edited, and advised with meticulous dedication and effort.

I solicited comments from many people on my book blog, and I thank all who gave feedback.

Julio Torres Lara, whom I met while living in Mexico, generously agreed to illustrate the cover for the book. His good nature and willingness to be part of the project is much appreciated.

Special thanks go to the crew of current and former students who, with good humor and hard work, helped me shape and produce both the ebook and print book. My initial brainstorming sessions with Matt Watson helped stretch my vision of an ebook. Evan Rowe worked tirelessly on the editing of the podcasts. Eric Arnold and Darrin Crescenzi advised me on technical questions.

Reid Parham was methodical and thorough in research. Michael John of Colorcubic created the music and kindly helped with final production of the podcasts. Ben Cerezo gave me valuable feedback as he and I worked on the initial design of the book. Kelli Reuther stepped in at the end to work diligently on design and production. A big thank you to the exceptional team, the "Wednesday night book group" of Anthony Armenda, Joe Carolina, Morgan Harrington, and Grace Noel, for countless hours of input and overall enthusiasm for the project.

My colleagues in design education are always an inspiration to me and I thank all who offered their projects for the book. In particular, I would like to thank Joshua Berger, Meredith Davis, Jessica Helfand, Steven Heller, and Warren Lehrer, for inspiring me with their pursuit of the written word.

On a more personal note, I would like to thank my family and friends for their continuous support. The constant encouragement and support of my parents for all I endeavor to do has made a huge difference in my life. Their passion for teaching helped me see at an early age the value of education.

So many wonderful people have touched my life, and among those dearest to me was my friend Sidney Rowe. Memories of her creative spirit will forever inspire me.

Index